Foundations of

WESLEYAN-ARMINIAN THEOLOGY

MILDRED BANGS WYNKOOP

D1121234

BEACON HILL PRESS
OF KANSAS CITY

FIRST PRINTING 1967

COPYRIGHT 1967 BY
BEACON HILL PRESS OF KANSAS CITY

PRINTED IN THE
UNITED STATES OF AMERICA

ISBN-13: 978-0-8341-0254-5
ISBN-10: 0-8341-0254-4

15   14   13

FOREWORD

By the time I became her pastor, Mildred Bangs Wynkoop was in her late 80s, stooped by the ravages of age and the effects of a stroke a decade or more earlier. She and her husband, Ralph, were faithful, supportive, and gracious members of the church. Rarely missing a Sunday service, they would come into the church with their faces radiant, with never a complaint, and quietly take their places about two-thirds of the way from the front.

Though advanced in years, Mildred was carefully attentive to every detail in a service. Her occasional notes of encouragement always spoke with appreciation for the music, the sermon, or some other element of the day. She especially loved Communion and would often send me notes of affirmation and appreciation for the service of the Lord's Table.

I had been appreciative of her writings for decades. Her *Theology of Love* had been the object of debate and conversation among pastors and theologians for many years, and she was a respected and thoughtful scholar. It was an honor to be her pastor for the last seven years of her life.

In 2005 I reread one of her earlier works, *Foundations of Wesleyan-Arminian Theology*. As I read it, I was struck once again by the careful scholarship of the book. In relatively few pages she captured the essential distinctive that is one of the foundation stones for the Wesleyan-Holiness tradition.

As I read it, I was impressed that this work deserves a new hearing. In an era when the dominant theological culture in North America is an evangelicalism that is predominantly Reformed and/or neo-Calvinistic, this work carves out a clear and articulate statement of the foundation on which our Wesleyan-Arminian theological tradition rests.

As she discusses her insight into the initiatives of God's grace and human responsibility, she provides the reader with a clear definition of the theological orientation that informed John and Charles Wesley in 18th-century England.

This movement gave rise to the massive influence of early Methodism on the frontiers in the development of North America.

In her clear and balanced wording, Dr. Wynkoop provides critical insight into the complex debates that gave rise to our theological tradition. She deserves to be read by a new generation of preachers, teachers, and laypersons. Her value to us is perhaps greater today than when this work was originally published. It is essential that we recover the tradition that provides a clear alternative to the predominance of theological perspectives at work in the popular evangelical culture.

I commend this work to the Church as worthy of a new and in-depth reading. May God give us a renewed vitality as we grasp the missional focus that stands firmly on a Wesleyan-Arminian theological foundation.

—Jesse C. Middendorf
General Superintendent, Church of the Nazarene

PREFACE

The controlling purpose of this study is to clarify and emphasize the doctrine of holiness. This is not a dogmatic approach. It is rather a historical study. Many threads of theological thought are properly and relevantly interwoven in this general subject, but so far as possible the contrast between (1) *the theory of particular predestination* and (2) *the Wesleyan concept of sanctification* will be lifted up for study.

Many of the objections to Wesleyan-Arminianism arise from the tension between these two points of view. Some misconceptions about holiness doctrine are rigid barriers against the doctrine though the source of the misconception is not recognized. Some "holiness preaching" perpetuates the antagonisms because of an ignorance of the cause of the tension. If this study can be even one step toward a mutual understanding, it will not have been in vain.

Though the single thread of predestination-sanctification will be the major line of study, it will be necessary to explore some of the immediately adjacent tangle of threads in order to keep a proper perspective. Many of these "sidelines" deserve far more extended treatment, but in this study each must be limited to its more direct relationship to the main subject. In fact this interest in perspective is germane to the study. It is our thesis that theological provincialism is precisely a lack of proper perspective and the failure to keep one's segment of truth in proper relationship to the full-orbed revelation.

The study begins with the history of the doctrinal development of the various theories of predestination and the controversies in which they were involved.

Predestination theories arose as a corrective to unguarded doctrines of the Church of God, and unbiblical concepts of grace and human nature. In the controversy, the proper goal of sanctification supported by the early Catholic church and Christian humanism was perverted. Predestination, then, in attempting to correct false views of the nature of the Church, gradually began to stand against the doctrine of sanctification (as later interpreted by Wesley), and finally has come to stand for a way of salvation exactly opposed to that represented by Wesleyan-Arminianism.

The next area of study centers around the characteristic theological tenets of Calvinism, high and low; Arminianism, evangelical and liberal; Wesleyanism, Wesleyan-Arminianism, and some varieties and combinations of these views.

The final section critically examines several theological tensions relevant to the subject of this study. The tensions exist because of the philosophical assumptions the Calvinist and Wesleyan-Arminian bring to the subjects under discussion. God's sovereignty and man's freedom are foundation stones to the theological structure. This in turn determines the meaning and relation of God's will and God's grace. Man's sin and God's grace are defined by whatever line of reasoning one follows in the previous steps. This leads inevitably to characteristic positions about divine decrees and salvation by faith, two mutually exclusive ways of salvation.

The conclusions arrived at to this point determine the concept one has of the work of the Holy Spirit in the life of the Christian and display the peculiar teachings characteristic of the two theological traditions very clearly. There are very practical consequences in life stemming from each view. The final step in theological logic is reached in theories of eternal security and assurance of salvation which, though antithetical to each other, answer to the same human need but each with its consequence in ethical concerns.

It is futile to debate sanctification against predestination or the witness of the Spirit against unconditional security or eradication against suppression, without a proper knowledge of and appreciation for the background of reasoning structuring each view. And defective concepts of the Wesleyan message of holiness as well as the accompanying defects in Christian grace are difficult to correct apart from this understanding.

In the case of Wesley's teaching it has been the author's judgment that the quoted passages should be documented by the titles of the specific sermon, essay, or letter. Since there are a number of editions of Wesley's works, not all available to every interested reader, it is presumed to be easier to find the passage by this means. In every case it has been our endeavor to draw from qualified sources for the substantiation of a position or the development of a thesis.

This study began to germinate into written form while I was teaching a few months in Taiwan in 1960. The lectures, given in English and interpreted into Mandarin Chinese, were taped and later published. A Japanese pastor acquired a copy, and translated it into the Japanese language and distributed it in mimeographed form. From this came a request to deliver the series of lectures in a more scholarly way to a Pastors' Retreat (the Japan Holiness church). After the lectures the desire was expressed for a more permanent type of publication. The research and enlargement which went into the preparation for this publication (to be translated into Japanese) became the foundation for this English book.

—MILDRED BANGS WYNKOOP

ACKNOWLEDGMENTS

The author is grateful to all publishers whose copyrighted material is quoted in these pages. Among these are Westminster Press (*Early Christian Fathers*, edited by Cyril Richardson); Muhlenberg Press (*A History of Christian Thought*, by J. L. Neve); Charles Scribner's Sons (*A History of Christian Thought*, by Arthur Cushman McGiffert); Wm. B. Eerdmans Publishing Co. (*Progress of Dogma*, by James Orr, and *Philosophy of the Christian Religion*, by Edward Carnell); Abingdon Press (*A Compend of Wesley's Theology*, edited by Burtner and Chiles); and, of course, Beacon Hill Press of Kansas City (*Christian Theology*, by H. Orton Wiley; *John Wesley's Concept of Perfection*, by Leo George Cox; *The Word and the Doctrine*, compiled by Kenneth E. Geiger; and *The Epistle to the Hebrews*, by H. Orton Wiley):

Appreciation is also expressed to the magazines *Christianity today* ("Debate over Divine Election," "Righteousness," by L. Nelson Bell, and "Arminius: An Anniversary Report," by Carl Bangs) and *Eternity* ("Eight Things God Cannot Do," by Donald Gray Barnhouse, and "Justification," by George E. Ladd).

Quotations from *The New English Bible* are by permission of the copyright owners, the Delegates of the Oxford University Press and the Syndics of the Cambridge University Press.

CONTENTS

Introduction

Our holiness heritage is very precious and sacred. The Wesleyan doctrine is not a theological emphasis whose major distinction is simply that it is different from Calvinism and that "holiness people" should be set apart from the mainstream of Christianity. *Holiness doctrine is central to all Christian faith.* It is thoroughly biblical and bears the stamp of the Church's approval from earliest Christian history.

It is a very "costly" doctrine, as all the major tenets of the Christian faith are. Our great Christian "Fathers," s e n s i t i v e to the needs of the Church, threshed out the theological problems involved and the verbal expressions best suited to understanding. They applied to the task all the zeal and grace and sanctified intelligence which were available. Great men, heroes, have died for their convictions.

Holiness doctrine is not an easy doctrine. It is not shallow or shoddy. It is not simply a moralism, a retreat from "the world," an escape from the humanness of man. It is not an emotionalism. There's blood on it, from the blood of Jesus on the cross of Calvary to the blood of heroes who counted the Word of God of more value than life itself. What these men believed powerfully influenced *their* lives—and influences *our* lives today. What we really believe about holiness powerfully influences *our* actions and choices, as well as influencing the lives of those to whom we minister and testify.

It is well to review the costliness of holiness doctrine that we may learn to treasure what we have received and put it to work in our lives. We must live it and preach it with understanding and with the same dedication and zeal and sacrifice and victory that characterized these who lived and died for their faith and for our spiritual enrichment.

As we critically observe the Christian Church we are made aware of differences among us that seem to divide us by the very doctrine which we have said holds us together. Christianity is centrally concerned with holiness. Yet theories about holiness occasion divisions within the family of Christians.

If this is a problem, it is precisely the reason behind this study. That there are different theories about sanctification is granted. The *reason* for the several theories is the area of our investigation. A directive toward personal assurance is the goal of the study.

There is no desire to drive any wider wedge than now exists between Christian groups which makes fellowship more difficult. We should pray for the removal of any wedges. Although this study will be critical in the sense of being investigative, analytical, and objective, it will have missed its purpose completely if it engenders any spirit of "heresy hunting" or bigotry or bitterness. The Christian witness has been seriously hurt by Christians who cannot love one another or who cannot share Holy Communion with Christians anywhere and everywhere.

The purpose of this study is: (1) to understand the reasons for our existence as a holiness body and by this understanding clarify our task and strengthen our witness. Without intelligent self-awareness, our purpose and goals become indistinct and are finally lost. The danger is not that we may cease to exist as a corporate body but that we may permit some superficial and unworthy motive to assume the ascendancy in our thinking and loyalty rather than the great central issues of the gospel.

(2) We must also understand our sister churches whose doctrine of salvation differs somewhat from ours. Mutual understanding does much to establish a basis of fellowship, and erases the suspicions and misinterpretations which drain away spiritual strength.

(3) We must be able to answer these questions: (a) Are the reasons for our existence as a holiness church and a holiness movement significant enough to warrant the time, effort, money, and personnel spent on its development and upkeep? (b) If so, what is that specific reason? What is our mission? These are practical questions, as well as theoretical questions. The theory is important because it directly influences our practical personal motivation, our conduct, our spirit, and our zeal.

(4) This study is also consistent with the spirit of John Wesley, if not with the entire stream of Christianity called Wesleyanism. Wesley was self-critical and a careful scholar, putting all his theories to the test of Scripture, traditional Christian teaching, and v a l i d Christian experience. When he was sure of his position, his concern was to emphasize truth and guard against error. Wesley did not propose a new theology but stressed the experiential dimension of Christian theology. Wherever he thought that some theological theory of Christianity gave men any excuse for failing to appropriate the full measure of God's grace, here and now, that theory needed to be corrected by God's Word. One of Wesley's concerns was that there was something biblically defective about the Calvinism of his day. But his polemic was doctrinal, never personal. It was fearless and forceful, but never bitter.

This "break" with Calvinism was not a break in Christian fellowship but a correction of what he believed to be a false interpretation of Scripture. The man who could so brilliantly pile argument upon argument against Calvin's doctrine of predestination ("Free Grace," "Predestination Calmly Considered," etc.) also said, "It is the duty of every Arminian preacher, First, never in public or in private, to use the word Calvinist as a term of reproach" ("What Is an Arminian?"). Wesley also exhorted his followers, "Beware of schism! of making a rent in the Church of Christ" (A Plain Account of Christian Perfection). The mark of a

Methodist, he said, was not to try to distinguish himself from other Christians, but only from those who were unbelievers. Methodists should be distinguished by a humble, Christian walk. He expressed it in these words: "Is thy heart right as my heart is with thine? I ask no further question. If it be, give me thy hand. For opinions, or terms, let us strive together for the faith of the gospel" (A "The Character of a Methodist").

But Wesley was aware of the theological problem raised in the Calvinist's mind by his preaching and he sought to answer these questions carefully, biblically, and coinvincingly. He said that, since God requires holiness in men, he could not be content until his people experienced God's full saving grace. Men needed to be faced with the crisis event which begins a life of spiritual victory.

We today need to understand the nature of this crisis and all that is involved in it. We need to understand our responsibility to the continuing walk with God which His Word requires. Calvinism and Wesleyanism differ at these vital points; therefore a careful study is necessary.

The dividing line between these two Christian traditions rests upon opposing theories of predestination. In fact, when the study gets under way it will be seen that theories about predestination, not predestination itself, are the watershed between them. The doctrine of predestination is the crossroads of such matters as God's sovereignty and man's responsibility, sin and grace, justification and sanctification, human faith, and the work of the Holy Spirit. But *theories* of predestination arise out of very much deeper considerations. We must, therefore, explore these more fundamental assumptions. The fact of predestination is a biblical teaching, but we need to ferret out the problems which have arisen because men have tried to formulate theories about these things.

It is particularly important to distinguish carefully between predestination and *personal* predestination. In the course of the development of Christian doctrine the theory that specific individuals were the objects of election arose rather than the manner of God's governance of history in a more general way. This is a crucial theological issue.

Our study, then, must begin with a brief history of how these theories of predestination arose. Where is the source of Calvin's theory of predestination? On what grounds did Wesley oppose it? What is the history of our own variant views of predestination as it relates to holiness? Holiness and predestination represent differing salvation theories in our theologies. Since both holiness and predestination are biblical doctrines, there should be no division of fellowship over them. It can only be prayerfully hoped that a bit of added light may be cast on a subject often darkened by emotional prejudice.

I *Background of the Doctrine of Personal Predestination*

EARLY CHRISTIAN ECUMENICITY

The early Christian Church as a whole was united along very clear and definite lines. The Early Church was not tightly organized as we know it today, but there was a sufficient unity of spirit and a common understanding of the Christian faith to agree on the great conclusions we now know as the ecumenical creeds regarding such matters as the nature of Christ, the

Trinity, and the canon of Scripture. These creeds were formulated to guard against the heresies on these matters which had been raised. These are standard Christian dogmas recognized by all Christians even today. "Both East [Eastern Othodox church] and West [early Catholic church] recognize four major Ecumenical Councils. . . . By 'ecumenical' is meant one which . . . is accepted by the entire Church as rightly representing it in its definitions of faith."[1]

The councils which gave their names to these creedal statements were:

1. Council of Nicaea (A.D. 325), affirming the true deity of Christ against Arius.

2. First Council of Constantinople (A.D. 381), affirming the true manhood of Christ against Apollinarius, and the personality of the Holy Spirit against Macedonius.

3. Council of Ephesus (A.D. 431), affirming the unity of Christ's person against the Nestorians.

4. Council of Chalcedon (A.D. 451), affirming the clear distinction between Christ's human and divine nature against Eutychus. This gave the Church a creedal statement on Christology which has stood the test of centuries.

DEVELOPMENT OF DIVISIONS

Divisions gradually began to develop in the Church. The Eastern church with its highly speculative approach to theology moved away from the more practical Western church until the theological and ecclesiastical break finally materialized. The Western church took the name "Catholic" or "universal." But it accommodated within itself the many small groups of Christians who recog-

[1]H. Orton Wiley, *Christian Theology* (Kansas City: Beacon Hill Press of Kansas City, 1940), I, 68.

nized the weaknesses and errors which crept into the Church. They irritated the conscience of the Church until reforms resulted. These "cathartic" or purifying movements exercised a wholesome control to the many improper emphases and the unguarded power politics within the Church. But finally Luther's "irritation" occasioned a change of policy toward all those who could not and would not blindly accept ecclesiastical authority.

At the time of the Reformation the Western Catholic church split into two major factions, the *Roman* Catholic church (which could not truly be "Catholic" any longer) and the Protestants. The division represented two conflicting concepts of the Church and its relation to salvation. The Roman Catholics said that the only way to Christ was through the Church. The Protestants said that men come into the Church through Christ. This difference of viewpoint has far-reaching implications in the basic teachings regarding salvation.

Protestantism began to develop some internal fractures on less important matters but matters which have left permanent scars. Though all Protestants agreed on the basic soteriological truths, the Lutherans and Calvinists found themselves divided more or less on the basis (1) of national lines (German and French), (2) concepts of the Eucharist (Luther held to the spiritual presence of Christ in the bread and wine, and the Calvinists tended toward a memorial relationship only), (3) the doctrine of the Church (Luther's realism clung to the Catholic view, minus the hierarchy, and Calvinism's nominalism tended toward a more democratic and individualistic concept).

In addition to these broad divisions were several independent groups known as "charismatic" groups whose concern was for a more vital and personal relationship to God rather than the formal authority of the organized and creed-bound churches. The contri-

bution of Arminius to this total situation is of great
importance to the later interrelating of the groups and
the softening of the rigid lines between the great Christian traditions. All of the "main-line" churches and most
of the larger "sects" can trace their *raison d'etre* some-
where within the complex of ideologies which underlies
this brief outline.

Basis of Divisions

These divisions and subdivisions are based largely
on different philosophies rather than on different experiences of grace or on biblical teaching. The role of
philosophy in this matter is of importance to our understanding of our own relationship to holiness doctrine.
A simple chart may illustrate the point.

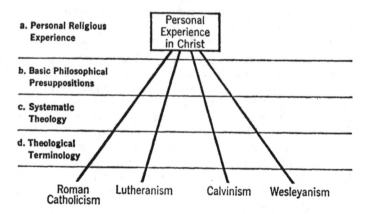

Level "a":

All Christians have the same experience of Christ.
We are all one in Him. For the sake of illustration we
have used the names of four representative Christian
traditions: Roman Catholicism, Lutheranism, Calvinism, and Wesleyanism. All m e m b e r s who "know

Christ" in their hearts know the *one Christ*. Only in Him can salvation be obtained. Whoever is "in Christ" is saved. At this level there is no difference between us.

Level "b":

Differences begin to appear as men attempt to explain what they know of Christ. What are assumed to be "self-evident" truths become the framework of our explanations. The problem lies in the fact that men do not agree as to what may constitute basic self-evident truths. The history of Christian doctrine is in some degree a history of the development and dominance of prevailing philosophies into which the Christian faith has been fitted. A shock always accompanies the emergence of a new philosophy into history, and certain features of Christian theology undergo more or less significant changes. A case in point is the way Thomas Aquinas boldly systematized Christian doctrine on Aristotle's logic and philosophical concepts. Theology had until then been strongly influenced by Neoplatonism. Thomas risked excommunication for his work but he is now called the "Father of Christian Theology." Today Christian doctrine is confronted by existentialism and "process" philosophy. Christian theology seeks a philosophical foundation adequate to its truth and congenial to the traditional way of thinking.

Level "c":

Systematic theology is Christian doctrine arranged according to principles inherent in whatever philosophy one accepts as foundational. That which is considered to be central to Christian theology assumes primary importance and all other doctrines follow logically from this premise. But major differences in theology become apparent at this point.

An interesting illustration of this phenomenon is the radical difference in theories of soteriology which arise from the several "orders of decrees" which various groups hold. The order in which the decrees are thought to follow one another are probably determined more by logical necessity than by clear biblical teaching, and yet the order of divine decrees constitutes some of the major divisions within Protestantism, as this study will show.

Level "d":

The words and terms which are used by all Christians are basically the same. In our illustration, Christians all speak of sin and grace, justification and sanctification, God's sovereignty and man's freedom, and all the other essential theological terms. But each of these terms is clothed with the inferences and connotations stemming from the basic philosophies of each group —philosophies which are seldom recognized as such but naively considered to be the common heritage of all rational minds. Communication and understanding seem to be blocked in every encounter between these groups. We "talk past each other" instead of engaging in meaningful dialogue. We often accuse each other of dishonesty and bigotry when the truth is that we each speak out of a narrow theological provincialism which blinds us to the provincialism of those to whom we speak. Let us trace the history of some of these provincialisms.

THEOLOGICAL PROVINCIALISM

We are using the term "provincialism" to mean any partial truth or any emphasis within the total Christian teaching which tends to obscure other factors of the whole, or which denies or rejects any part of the whole. Lifting one aspect of doctrine into a central dominating position, away from its proper place in the whole doctrine, is provincialism. Such theological provincialisms are not necessarily untruths but they invariably distort the Christian gospel because they, apart from the whole gospel, are made to become themselves the judge of truth and actually the gospel. The Christian gospel, as presented in the Scriptures, is the Word of God. No part can be neglected, and no part can, itself, become the whole without betraying the gospel. A fine, sensitive, and proper balance of all sides of biblical teaching is the great contemporary need.

The New Testament Christian Church believed and taught that Christ died for all men. They said that any man could be saved by turning to the Saviour in faith. They seemed not to question the God-given ability of any and all men to respond to God's invitation. This confidence was reflected in the tremendous evangelistic and missionary impetus in the Pentecostal Church. The Church grew and spread as fire in a dry forest. Poor churches sent their best leaders as missionaries (Acts 13:1-3), and followed the giving of choice men with gifts of money and material to churches more needy than themselves. This was joyously and spontaneously done (II Cor. 8:1-5).

The "Apostolic Fathers" (i.e., Barnabas, Clement, Ignatius, Polycarp, and others) were those Christian leaders who immediately followed the New Testament apostles and were supposedly taught by them. They believed and taught that the human will is free to choose good or evil, God or sin. Whereas all the New Testament literature was written by Jews, that which followed came almost exclusively from Gentile pens. Vital Christianity was almost wholly Gentile after the death of the apostles.

Immediately following the apostolic age, as the young Gentile churches were forced to face a pagan society without the leadership of those who had personally known Christ, two sources of opposition required attention: (1) the pagan attack and (2) internal schism. "The unity of the Church around its leaders and the preservation of the faith from perversion are the dominant themes. In consequence, the religious spontaneity of the New Testament writings gives place to a more moral and ecclesiastical note."[2] The deep spiritual concern of the New Testament is modified in these writings but there is an intense interest in the basic gospel message. But facing, as these early Christians were, the dangers of apostasy in a pagan society, a great deal of attention was given to proper behavior, repentance, ecclesiastical form, and proper belief. They taught salvation, not so much by faith as by merit. There was an overemphasis on ethics to the neglect of grace and personal Christian experience. Neve says that "there is scarcely any trace of the doctrine of justification in the writings of those fathers."[3] Neve quotes Clement as saying (*Homily of Clement,* XVI, 4), "Almsgiving is excellent as a repentance for sins; fasting is better than prayer; but almsgiving is better than either,—for almsgiving becomes a lightening of the burden of sins." And he quotes from Hermas (*Similitude,* V, 3, 3) as follows: "If you can do more than that God commands, you will earn more glory for yourself and you will have more honor before God."[4]

THE PELAGIAN-AUGUSTINIAN CONTROVERSY

Pelagius

In A.D. 409, a British monk by the name of Pelagius came to Rome. He was a man of high character and known for his personal sanctity. A. C. McGiffert says of him: "He was profoundly interested in Christian conduct and devoted himself to the task of improving

[2]Cyril Richardson, ed., *Early Christian Fathers* (Philadelphia: Westminster Press, 1943), p. 17.

[3]J. L. Neve, *A History of Christian Thought* (Philadelphia: The Muhlenberg Press, 1946), I, 38.

[4]*Ibid.*, p. 39.

moral conditions in the local community which seemed to him in sad need of change for the better. He had a large following and wielded considerable influence as a religious and moral leader. In accordance with the best Christian tradition he laid emphasis particularly on personal purity and abstinence from the corruptions and frivolities of the world. While he was not an extreme ascetic his teaching was rigorous and he made a strong appeal to the more serious-minded in the church."[5]

Pelagius felt that the undue emphasis Tertullian gave to original sin had a tendency to undermine a sense of personal responsibility. McGiffert continues: "The doctrine of original sin he wholly rejected, insisting that sin is purely voluntary and individual and cannot be transmitted. Adam's fall affected neither the souls nor the bodies of his descendants. Their flesh comes from him but not their souls, and their flesh is good as everything made by God is good. So far as their nature and abilities go, all human beings are in the same condition as Adam was in the beginning. They suffer, however, from the bad example of the race as he did not. In spite of this they are free, as he was free, and are able freely to choose either good or evil. Like Adam every man creates his own character and determines his own destiny. His character belongs to him and cannot be handed on to another. Moreover his character does not determine his conduct. He is able to change his course of action whenever he so desires."[6]

Only a few fragments of Pelagius' writings have been preserved. Most of what we know of his writings has been included in Augustine's works, and in the works of Pelagius' disciples who added rationalistic and

[5]Arthur Cushman McGiffert, *A History of Christian Thought* (New York: Charles Scribner's Sons, 1953), II, 125.

[6]*Ibid.*, p. 126.

naturalistic elements. From these sources we may summarize his teaching as follows: Adam was created
mortal and death is the natural expectation of all men.
Death is not punishment for sin. Man's will is absolutely
free. By making use of his natural ability he may choose
good over evil freely. If God demanded obedience
to His law He must have given man power to obey.
There is no bias toward sin in the human heart—no inbred sin carried in the race. No man's sin can affect
another; Adam's sin could not affect the whole race.

Pelagius was well aware that most men did sin
and would suffer punishment eternally. Sinners need
to be saved and Christ came to save sinners and was
our Example and Inspiration for Christian living.

"Though Pelagius made so much of human ability
and independence he yet talked about the necessity of
divine grace, insisting that without it no one can win
eternal life. He meant by divine grace, however, not
some indwelling divine power or substance, but instruc-
tion and enlightenment. He even used the word grace
in a still broader sense to denote free will and the gifts
of reason and conscience with which all men are endowed."[7]

Pelagius had gone to Rome but it is very doubtful
that he had heard of Augustine until political problems
in Rome made it agreeable for him and his follower
Coelestius to go to Carthage, where Augustine's influence was very great. From 411 o n w a r d, the
controversy between the two men was increasingly
pronounced. Eventually Pelagius went east and made
his home in Palestine, where his views became popular
and where Augustine's views never could get a foothold.
But Augustine carried on the controversy in the form of
many published essays.

Pelagius summed up in his theological position that

which became the major theological tenets of the Eastern church. The speculative nature of the Eastern mind tended toward an undue emphasis on man's freedom and perfectibility. Eastern thought lost the deep sense of guilt and sin, and hence, of grace.[8] Wiley feels that the great controversy between Augustine and Pelagius was in a much more fundamental sense "a conflict between the East and the West [as] focused in these eminent theologians."[9]

Augustine

Pelagius' theories were challenged by the most influential single person in the Christian Church since the Apostle Paul, namely, Augustine (354-430). The controversy has divided the Church ever since. Augustine's personal history undoubtedly had something to do with his theology. His personal talents and intelligence were magnificent and his genius for apologetics was equal to the occasions he met in his lifetime. He became a Christian almost against his will out of a very evil life. He never lost the wonder of the overwhelming power of grace and his mother's prayers to reverse his life direction.

His searching mind had explored all the leading philosophical tendencies of his age and "he was influenced by so many currents of thought which he failed to synthesize into one harmonious whole that contradictions are frequently met."[10] He never fully recovered from Neoplatonic dualism. Yet he asserted human worth against the Manichaean's concept of degraded human nature, and affirmed human depravity

[8]James Orr, *Progress of Dogma* (Grand Rapids: Wm. B. Eerdmans Publishing Co., 1952), p. 26.

[9]*Op. cit.,* p. 69.

[10]A. W. Nagler, *The Church in History* (New York: Abingdon-Cokesbury Press, 1929), p. 74.

against the Pelagian over-idealized natural human ability. In fact, quite contradictory streams of theological thought issued from Augustine's teaching—ecclesiastical authority which the Roman Catholic church built upon, and his mysticism and doctrine of grace typical of Protestantism.

The sharp contrast between Pelagius' and Augustine's views created an exaggerated tension, and in the heat of controversy both men proposed doctrines to refute the other and to support their own that were more extreme than would normally have been the case. Controversy creates a wholesome critical atmosphere but it is beset by the danger of extremism rather than merely the correction of errors. Certainly the followers of Pelagius systemized some features of his views in a way that makes history remember him for a position which he himself probably did not hold.[11] And Augustine was driven to logical conclusions which subsequent study of his teachings prove to be inconsistent with his own more mature views.

It is interesting to summarize and compare the views of Pelagius and Augustine.

Pelagius taught:

1. Man has a perfectly free will. He can do what God requires him to do.

2. There is no innate impulse to sin, no original sin inherited from Adam.

3. Sin is the simple choice to do wrong. Man's sensual nature is the occasion, not the cause, of sin.

4. Grace, as a cause, is unnecessary to move the will toward God. Christ acts as an Example and motivation to right acting. Christian perfection is only a

[11]Cf. Neve, *op. cit.,* I, 143.

cluster of individual virtues and works with no demand for a regenerated heart.

Augustine rejected this and affirmed:

1. God created man *posse non peccare et non mori* (possible not to sin and die). The will was master.

2. Man misused his freedom and willed to disobey God. As a consequence he entered the state of *non posse non peccare et mori* (not possible not to sin and die) because God no longer gave direction to the will.

3. The will became a sinning will. All men share in this evil will because all men were in Adam when he sinned and hence sinned with him. All are guilty.

4. Salvation (here Augustine failed to see his own ambiguity) is only by

a. Baptism, which assures a child of s a l v a t i o n —hence he favored infant baptism; or

b. Grace, which is absolutely necessary for salvation, because only grace can move man's will.

Our task at this point is not to trace the history of the Pelagian-Augustinian controversy. It is sufficient to note the logical form of Augustine's reasoning which was developed "out of an inner need for the assurance of salvation,"[12] and in contrast to his antagonist, Pelagius.

Notice the logical development of his reasoning:

1. God is absolutely sovereign. He is the direct cause of all that is. No one can stand against His will. (This is his premise and it reflects a Neoplatonic view of God as wholly other, unknown, unapproachable.)

2. Fallen man, therefore, is absolutely powerless to will anything against God, or for Him. In contrast to God's holiness, man is utterly evil.

[12]*Ibid.,* I, 147.

3. If any man is saved and turns to God, it is only because God has moved man's will to respond to Him; that is, God changes the inclination of the heart so that the man acts in freedom. Grace changes the heart. But in the work of changing the heart grace acts in such a way that man's will cannot resist. We can say, as Neve puts it, that man is converted, not because he wills, but he wills because he is converted.[13]

4. Grace is irresistible because God's will is irresistible. Therefore whom God would save will be saved, and he will not ever be lost because it is God who takes the responsibility for moving his will and God cannot change.

5. If Christ died for *all* men, as some were saying, all men would be saved. *But,* he observed,

6. Not all men are saved. Why? (In Augustine's earlier years he answered this question by reference to man's free agency, not by electing grace.[14])

7. Obviously not all men are saved because God must have chosen *particular* men to salvation, a specific number of men which cannot be changed. The rest are left in their sins. It is inconceivable that Christ should die for anyone who would not be saved.

8. Since God cannot change, it is only reasonable to suppose that elect men were chosen from all eternity.

9. Therefore individual predestination is the only logical way to account for the salvation of any man.

Personal predestination, to Augustine, was not a biblical doctrine but the inevitable conclusion to his own line of reasoning, which he believed was biblical. His logic compelled him to make God fully responsible for the salvation of certain pre-chosen men. His doctrine of predestination was not an *a priori* but a conclusion.

---

[13]*Ibid.*
[14]Cf. Wiley, *op. cit.,* II, 234.

It must be also said that Augustine refused to follow his own logic to its inevitable conclusion and to make God the author of sin or the cause of any man's damnation. This step his followers would take in later years.

In this way Augustine arrived at the doctrine of personal predestination. This was not, as noted above, a teaching which he found from a study of the Bible, but the conclusion to his own logic and which he then believed had to be biblical. Augustine's doctrine of personal predestination was developed *after* he developed his doctrine of sin and grace.[15]

His concept of grace as acting directly on the human will "necessitated a belief in a divine decree which determined the exact number of those who were to be saved. . . . From these views . . . there gradually grew up a theory of predestination."[16]

An Analysis

It has been observed that Augustine's theory of predestination makes the divine decrees the prime cause of salvation and Christ's death a subsidiary and secondary cause. Certainly salvation by divine decree and salvation by faith in Christ's meritorious death on the Cross are two very different things. In the first case, Christ is not absolutely essential to salvation but is only a link in a predetermined chain of events. In the second case, Christ is absolutely essential to salvation and from Him stream the benefits of the atonement. The latter seems a better interpretation of Scripture.

To serve the purpose of this study it is of value to observe that the truly great Augustine was Christian and intelligent enough not to permit his proclamation of the gospel to be limited by his own logic. He preached to men as if they were capable of exercising free moral

[15]Cf. Neve, *op. cit.*, I, 146.
[16]Wiley, *op. cit.*, II, 348-49.

choice, as he had yielded his own evil heart to his
mother's beloved Saviour. His writings teach that men
may respond to God's call in order to be converted.
But, also, he taught that men can be saved only by
receiving baptism from the Church. He taught the need
for infant baptism to assure salvation to all.

This leaves us with some puzzling questions (1)
Are men saved by divine decree predetermined in
the secret counsel of God's inscrutable will? (2) Is
man saved by the Church's baptism? (3) Or is he
saved by faith in Christ? These are mutually exclusive
ways of salvation, yet Augustine taught them all without intellectual embarrassment. In fact Augustine was
"not able to carry out logically his scheme of predestination, for he had no solution of the difficulty that
electing grace should be bound up with a sacramental
system of external ordinances."[17]

So great a Christian thinker was he that almost
the entire Christian Church has found some ground
in his teachings upon which to build great systems of
doctrine. But these systems when projected into independent theological forms exclude one another because each is built upon a *segment* of doctrine unrelated
to the larger comprehension of truth which surged
through the mind of the man who is considered to be
the greatest Christian teacher subsequent to the apostles.
The resulting doctrinal systems are incompatible because each declares a view of salvation contradictory to
the others, and this contradiction becomes a barrier
to unity and fellowship. These theological divisions in
the Christian Church are based on *logical* contradictions
in a large measure rather than upon biblical exegesis,
and this point is significant to the study under consideration.

It should be noted that Augustine's extreme view

[17]*Ibid.*, p. 349.

of personal predestination was rejected by the Church. A so-called semi-Pelagianism prevailed. Augustine's views were revived in the ninth century by the monk Gottschalk, but again the Church resolutely cast them aside. Gottschalk saw the dangers in the semi-Pelagianism of the Church but his worthy attempt at restoration of salvation by grace alone was weakened by his failure to acknowledge any kind of human freedom, psychological or formal. Because of this extreme position he opened the door to antinomianism, and a possible breakdown of the whole ecclesiastical system of the Church. Several synods were held in an attempt to resolve the tension between the two positions, and a mediating position prevailed again over extreme predestination in favor of practical piety.[18]

By way of summary and conclusion, it should be noted that Pelagius and Augustine were each attempting to preserve valid truths. Pelagius was concerned about preserving human dignity and moral responsibility, which was necessary and proper to do. Augustine wanted to preserve the absolute sovereignty of God and the absolute need for His grace in relation to salvation, which was also right. But in the tension of controversy a false antithesis was forced between these two points of view. Each man, in overemphasizing his truth, tended to lose the opposite correcting or complementary truth. Pelagius lost the need for God's grace and Augustine lost the concept of true moral responsibility.

In relation to our study of predestination and holiness it must be noted that personal predestination by divine decree was not originally intended to be a challenge to the doctrine of holiness but a doctrine to preserve the majesty and sovereignty of God against the danger of making man independent of Him. But in-

[18]Neve, *op. cit.*, I, 179.

herent in the theory of personal predestination is a denial of the possibility of practical holiness as Wesley understood it. The doctrine of personal predestination challenges the Wesleyan doctrine of sanctification at its heart.

In his sermon "Free Grace," Wesley said:

If [election] be so, then is all preaching vain. It is needless to them that are elected; for they whether with preaching or without, will infallibly be saved. Therefore, the end of preaching—to save souls—is void in regard to them; and it is useless to them that are not elected, for they cannot possibly be saved: They, whether with preaching or without, will infallibly be damned. . . .

This, then, is a plain proof that the doctrine of predestination is not a doctrine of God, because it makes void the ordinance of God; and God is not divided against himself. A Second is, that it directly tends to destroy that holiness which is the end of all the ordinances of God . . . The doctrine [of election] . . . has a tendency to destroy holiness in general; for it wholly takes away those first motives to follow after it . . . the hope of future reward and punishment, the hope of heaven and the fear of hell.[19]

[19]John Wesley, *Sermons.*

II *The Development of the Doctrine of Personal Predestination*

AUGUSTINE'S CONCEPTS

The Catholic church followed Augustine's teaching regarding the Church as being the only door to God's grace and eternal salvation. Salvation by the sacraments gradually lead to an overemphasis on the total power and authority of the Church and its hierarchy. "Salvation only through the Church" came to mean the total submission of the conscience of each individual to the dictates of the Church. This was only one step from the arbitrary, unbiblical, and sometimes immoral abuses of the system of "indulgences" which tied the individual to the Church, hand, foot, heart, and purse, and encouraged him in his sins.

Certainly Augustine should not be held responsible for the abuses of the Catholic church. Had not Luther rebelled, it would not be hard to imagine Augustine himself returning from the dead to do what Luther did. Again, the logic of the Augustinian concept of the Church, uncorrected by his total contribution, led into the abuse of the system of indulgences.

In the sixteenth century, Martin Luther and later John Calvin called the Church back to the biblical doctrine of justification by faith in Christ. Basically their reaction was to the Church's arrogant, self-appointed sovereignty over the souls of men w h i c h robbed God of His absolute sovereignty. Probably the indulgence problem became the *occasion* for the conflict rather than the *cause* of it. The question really was, Who is to be God? The Reformers did not intend to create a new church or new doctrines. They called the Church back to its own governing doctrines which they believed were being desecrated by the Catholic church. Luther wished to reform the Church, not split it.

Augustine's intellectual leadership furnished the philosophical foundation for the Reformation, particularly his concept of the sovereignty of God. Salvation by the sovereign God's eternal decree and only on God's initiative stood squarely against the Church's teaching that salvation could be obtained only through obedience to the decrees of the Church and by the accummulation of merit through good works or the payment of money.

The biblical doctrine of salvation by faith alone, which challenged the Catholic doctrine of salvation by works, rested on the deeper issue of God's sovereignty. It is here that Augustine's concept of God prevailed in Protestantism and salvation by divine decree became the orthodox position.

But this raised a new question: Are we saved by divine decree or by faith? Or, to state it in a more recognizable form, Are we saved by grace alone (Augustine's concept of grace as a divine cause) or by faith alone? Both *sola gracia* and *sola fides* were Protestant affirmations. The logical problem was easily and quickly solved by arbitarily making faith subservient to grace: God gives elect men a special kind of faith for salvation. In this way predestination was given priority over every other doctrine and became the controlling principle of Reformation theology. Because of it, the biblical concept of faith was changed to fit into the doctrine of personal predestination. Thus Augustine's logical conclusion—personal predestination—becomes the principle of biblical interpretation instead of biblical exegesis becoming the basis of theology.

CALVIN'S CONCEPT OF PERSONAL AND DOUBLE PREDESTINATION

In noting Calvin's contribution to the Church in general and to the Reformation in particular, we must remember that he was trying to bring Christian doctrine and practical life into clear focus in the confused minds of people who had only recently broken away from the absolute authority of the Catholic church. They had learned to obey in the Catholic church but not to think. "Gospel freedom" could be (and was among some) interpreted to mean irresponsible freedom. Few people could read anything, let alone the Bible and theology books which were in Latin. The few existing handwritten Bibles were chained to tables in the churches for the scholars to read. Laymen could "read theology only in ritual and church architecture.

The people needed firm guidance in theology and social behavior from their leaders. By the time of the Reformation the Bible was available in the vernacular, but its interpretation and application to life were defective as well as inadequate. Fanciful, allegorical interpretation had been inherited from earlier ages and needed to be challenged and corrected—a major task, never fully accomplished.

Calvin's greatest challenge, perhaps, was to furnish leadership in this situation. Trained in law, and with a logical cast of mind, he was eminently suited to the task. His *Institutes of the Christian Religion* is a theological masterpiece. It began as a very simple and brief explanation of the Creed.[1] Simple people could memorize it and cling to its message.

After a number of editions, each more complete than the previous one, it took the form we now have. But with all its enlargement, the simple, clear statements of the Creed stand out like the limbs of a tree. And as it was expanded, the logic-controlled contents began to shine like polished gems. Its structure aids the memory; its logic satisfies the mind. The *Institutes* took the place of authority in the Protestant world which the Church had once had. In the Preface to the 1559 edition of the *Institutes*, Calvin says that the principles and methods outlined and applied in the book should become the principle of biblical interpretation. "My design in this work has been to prepare and qualify students of theology for the reading of the divine word . . . and to proceed in it without any obstruction. For I think I have given such a comprehensive summary, and orderly arrangement . . . that, with proper attention, no person will find any difficulty in determin-

[1]John Calvin, "Syllabus," *Institutes of the Christian Religion,* trans. John Allin (6th Amer. ed.; Philadelphia: Presbyterian Board of Christian Education, 1932), I, 41.

ing what ought to be the principal objects of his search in the Scripture."[2]

In examining the *Institutes* it is obvious that the doctrines systematized in them are not exegetically determined. Scripture is used to illuminate and give authority to the doctrines. Calvin's grasp of the essential truths of the Bible is enormous and impressive but it is obvious that the philosophical system underlying theology has taken precedence over exegetical considerations. Calvin did not reject exegesis. Exegesis, as we now know it, had not been developed. Calvin's contribution is an appeal to Scripture as authority.

But we must examine Calvin's teaching. Calvin built on Augustine's philosophy. But *Calvin's premise was Augustine's conclusion.* Augustine's reasoning led him to the conclusion that God predestines some men to salvation. Augustine would carry his logic no further. Calvin carried Augustine's reasoning one step further. If God is absolutely sovereign and He predestines some men to salvation, it is only reasonable to suppose that He also predestines all other men to damnation. Thus was revived in the Church, Gottschalk's teaching of "double predestination." Augustine drew back from an emphasis on "election to damnation" (though he probably taught it). Calvin's logical and honest mind was forced to affirm it, but he, like Augustine, drew back from carrying the logic beyond this point. Both men were dedicated and vital Christians before they were theoreticians.

The theory of personal predestination was not, then, derived from biblical exegesis but was a doctrine demanded by logical necessity to defend the absolute sovereignty of God a g a i n s t the sovereignty of the Church. And predestination to damnation was a natural and logical development from an accepted premise.

2*Ibid.*

Calvin develops his doctrine of predestination in Book III, chapter 21A, of the *Institutes*. In this section he tries to answer the questions which arise about the goodness of God when He saves some and refuses to save others. His answers center around the "foolishness" of mere man attempting to "penetrate the inner recesses of divine wisdom."[3] We should not be "ashamed to be ignorant" but "abstain with cheerfulness from the pursuit of that knowledge." But one must not "withhold from believers" what the Scripture clearly teaches about predestination. Not all Calvinists proved to be this humble, and perhaps this humility might be increased in much of our own thinking.

The "second degree of election" is election to damnation.[4] But yet another dimension is needed to round out this truth, namely, particular election, or the election of specific individuals. God "not only offers salvation but assigns it in such a manner that the certainty of the effect is liable to no suspense or doubt."[5]

Joseph Haroutunian, in class lectures at Garrett Biblical Institute (summer school, 1950) reminded the students that Calvin's doctrine of predestination and election represented a final repudiation of the Catholic doctrine of good works and merit. The "Horrible Decree," as Wesley quoted Calvin regarding it, must be understood in the context of the history of the development and meaning of the doctrine.

Calvin was no more consistent than Augustine. Though his system was logical—said to be one of the most logical theologies ever written—his preaching and biblical exegesis and social theory allowed for a greater

[3]*Ibid.*, bk. III, par. 1.

[4]*Ibid.*, pars. 6 and 7.

[5]*The Poetical Works of John and Charles Wesley*, G. Osborn, ed. (London: Wesleyan Methodist Conference Office, Paternoster-Row, 1869), III, 34 ff.

measure of human moral responsibility than his theology could defend. As was Augustine, he was a better Christian than theologian.

In the theological vacuum of the sixteenth century, Protestant schools for training ministers became a very pressing need. A number of schools were established, each taking a somewhat different view of predestination. The Church had never agreed on any one theory of predestination. The rigid forms had failed to appeal to any large segment of Protestantism. The milder and more flexible Belgic Confession and the Heidelberg Confession came as near to "orthodoxy" as was possible. When the supralapsarian interpretation of these creeds was advocated, many intellectuals feared a "new papacy" forming in the clergy would undermine the freedom of the Church. The problem of predestination did not begin with Calvin nor was it limited to purely theological concerns. Involved in the predestination controversy was the problem of toleration in religion, politics, ecclesiology, and society in general.

Scholarly Calvin established a university in Geneva, Switzerland, to train ministers. Young men came from all over Europe, but particularly from the low countries, to study there. In this way Calvin's theology spread rapidly and widely over Europe. Calvin himself filled the chair of theology. When he died, one of his students, Theodore Beza, took Calvin's place in the university as theology professor. From this time a distinction must be made clearly between Calvin's own views and *Calvinism* which was developed through his followers and which took several lines. Calvin would not recognize all the teachings that now go under the name Calvinism. (Nor would Wesley approve of all the Wesleyanism extant today.) As with the case of all great leaders, their disciples usually fail to grasp the whole scope of truth which the master saw. Segments of truth, or major emphases divorced from the total concept, are raised to central prominence. So there develops several "Paulinisms," or Calvinisms or Wesleyanisms, even Buddhisms and Mormonisms. In evaluating modern Christian movements, it is necessary to understand this principle.

DOUBLE PREDESTINATION AND DIVINE DECREES

Beza became the mastermind of the Geneva University. His interpretation of Calvin's teaching influenced Calvinism all over Europe through the ministerial students who came to study there.

Beza carried Reformation logic another inevitable step. Both Augustine and Calvin were too devotedly Christian and realistic to permit their reasoning to proceed to its ultimate conclusions. Augustine's belief in a *loving* God was satisfied by the conclusion that God's decrees assure salvation for the elect. Calvin was too "intoxicated" with love for a *just* God to go further than his double-predestination theory. Since no man deserves salvation, God is not unfair to save some and damn others. Even the soul in hell should rejoice that he has been personally selected by a most gracious God to his particular destiny. In some way God's glory is revealed by His decrees even in hell. God is just and righteous.

But Beza's sharp and logical mind was not arrested by this same love of God, so characteristic of Augustine and Calvin. He saw only that if God is absolutely sovereign and man is helpless in sin, and that men are saved or damned by God's decree, therefore it must be concluded that God *causes* men to sin just as He causes men to be saved. This was not a new doctrine with Beza, but a hidden element inherent in the whole approach to theology stemming from Augustine. Neither Augustine nor Calvin foresaw this nor would they likely have approved it when expressed in that way.

Beza's logic is reflected in his "order of God's decrees," which is known as the supralapsarian view. This view implies that sin, being necessary to implement the divine decrees regarding the damnation of some men, must also have been decreed by God prior to the other decrees. This extreme predestination doctrine was now taught in the Geneva University as orthodox Calvinism. The pastors of some Reformed churches taught this doctrine in contradiction to the milder wording of the Belgic Confession, which had been accepted as orthodox by most Calvinistic churches.

Two factors must be noted about Beza's "Calvinism." First, he subscribed to a specific sequence of divine decrees. This sequence of decrees supported the extreme theological position he held. Second, he presumed to know, apart from biblical teaching, what the correct order was. This was not in keeping with Calvin's expressed opinion regarding man's knowledge about God. That there were other "orders," with other theological conclusions without any better or worse biblical justification, testifies to the instability of this method of building foundations under theological systems.

Wesleyans do not usually speak of the decrees of God. In other Protestant traditions "divine decrees" serve a very important f u n c t i o n in theology. The order which the decrees are thought to be related to each other determines the distinctive emphasis of each tradition. Though Wesleyans are not always aware of the way in which the Calvinistic theology is structured by a concept of decrees, it seems obvious that there is a definite relationship between this "order" and the consequent teaching on soteriology.

Among those who build theology on the decrees, it is observed that there are several so-called divine decrees, or elements, in God's purpose for the world, and the method of achieving that purpose. This plan was determined in the prehistorical secret councils of the Godhead. Among the decrees are those having to do with the time sequence of creation, the Fall, and salvation. The curious thing is that there is a real and significant difference of opinion about the proper order of these decrees. The difference of opinion arises at the point where the problem of God's knowledge is debated. Is God's knowledge predictive or does God simply foreknow what man will do? If God foreknows, how does He know an event that has not occurred if the agent of that event is genuinely free? Would not such a contingency limit the sovereignty of God?

The *supralapsarian* system puts the decree to elect some men to salvation and to reprobate all others before the decree to create them. *Infralapsarianism* puts the decree to create all men before the decree to permit the Fall, which in turn is followed by the "decree" to provide salvation. *Sublapsarianism* understands the decree to provide salvation to follow (1) creation, (2) the Fall, and (3) personal election. There are significant implications to the differences in these systematizations.

Arminius observed that in some systems Christ was made secondary and virtually unnecessary by these decrees in whatever order some of them appear. Men are saved, not by Christ, according to this, but by God's decree or will. In them, moreover, the provision for salvation appears to be an afterthought on God's part. In order to account for the Christ-event one is forced to assume a fundamental antagonism within God's nature, between His holiness and love, between His justice and mercy, between His will and His permission.

To resolve this i m p o s s i b l e contradiction it is necessary to put the moral integrity of God back behind the veil of human understanding and say, "God cannot be called to account for His immutable and inscrutable purpose. Who are we, weak worms of the dust, to say what God can or cannot do or what God ought or ought not to do?"

And yet it is precisely the moral nature of God, as He reveals it, that gives us the only clue to any moral rightness that we may know. Are we to be more just than God, or may we make God conform to some universal moral order outside of God? Is it necessary to defend God for His failure to conform to a moral order we set up?

The solution is to look once again behind the curtain of history to find out if possible what God's purpose was in creation. We need to be reminded, however, that where revelation is silent we ought not to presume to speak. This does not mean that we are to remain in ignorance. "The Lamb slain before the foundation of the world" points the way to postulating a "decree," if such a word is proper, which puts Christ in the very center of human existence. He is not only the creative Word of God, but He is the Fountainhead of God's love and redemptive grace. Love is fundamentally sacrificial, and the love that prompted the creation of intelligences who could return that affection was also a love that could and would and does forgive, and redeem man at the terrible cost of personal suffering. But back of creation was the personal love of a personal God expressed through the second Person of the Godhead. *This is grace*—original grace that preceded original sin, and anticipated it. Prevenient grace, for that is our theological word for it, is not an afterthought but is the gracious outpouring of God's love surrounding every step of the history of mankind from the first flicker of intelligent life to the last flicker of human existence in history.

An interesting and important complication arose in regard to Calvinism. As the political hold of Roman Catholicism was giving way in the low countries, Calvinism as a *political* power gained ground. The *Confessions* became a sort of charter under which a group of Christian people were permitted the right to exist as a church. The *Confessions* defined the peaceful nature of the group and usually prevented persecution and tended to moderate political interference. But in the low countries it was not simply Calvinism, but Beza's *interpretation* of Calvinism, that defined religious orthodoxy to an important degree. Hence, to challenge Beza's interpretation of Calvinism was to challenge the political structure of the country and constituted treason against the government. Into this confused and complex situation stepped A r m i n i u s, who, as a good Calvinist himself, challenged an unbiblical interpretation of predestination. This challenge struck at the heart of a "rivalry between Dutch military and civil leaders. Religion and politics were inextricably interwoven in this country."[6]

The fact of this rivalry need only be noted in this short study, but the full story of it is essential to an adequate understanding of Arminiamism. Eventually some Arminians were to suffer execution as traitors instead of merely challengers of Beza's theological position. The ambiguous and emotional rejection of the Arminians by the Calvinists brought on by this confusion of religious with political interests carries over into theological differences today. Much of the contemporary attitude toward evangelical Arminianism among Calvinists would end if the real nature of the original conflict were better understood.

ARMINIUS' CONCEPT OF DIVINE DECREES

James Arminius was born in Oudewater, Holland, in 1560. His widowed mother was forced by economic necessity to let young James be placed in the care of others. He was adopted by a converted Catholic priest

------

[6]A. W. Harrison, *Arminianism* (London: Duckworth Press, 1937), p. 23.

who sent him to school in Utrecht. On the death of the priest, a professor at Marburg took the brilliant boy to the Lutheran University there. Within a short time the Spaniards took Oudewater and murdered most of the inhabitants because they refused to return to the Catholic faith. Among those killed were the mother and brothers and sister of Arminius. Bitterness for such ruthless political intolerance filled his heart and probably accounts for his resistence to the religious intolerance which he was to experience later.

The sad and homelsss boy found refuge in the home of Peter Bertius, pastor of the Reformed church at Rotterdam, who sent him to the new university at Leyden. Here he won distinction as a scholar. Finally the patrons of the great Amsterdam church "adopted" him, assuring him of the best possible education in exchange for his promise that he would return to them as pastor if this became their will. Briefly, Arminius was sent to the Geneva University for ministerial training, where he studied theology under Beza and others. There is some question as to whether Arminius ever accepted Beza's view, but he at least became thoroughly familiar with his "high Calvinist" position.[7]

At the conclusion of Arminius' education in Geneva, he was installed as pastor of the Amsterdam church. He was a brilliant preacher, a gifted Bible exegete, and a humble and dedicated Christian. He was particularly noted for his expository messages, and his popularity as a preacher brought many people to hear him.

In 1589 an educated layman, Mr. Koornheert, in Holland, raised a storm in theological circles by his scholarly lectures and writings in refutation of Beza's supralapsarian theory of the divine decrees. It is significant of the widely held dissatisfaction with the position

[7]Carl Bangs, "Arminius and the Reformation," *Church History*, Vol. XXX, No. 2, June, 1961, pp. 7-8.

of Calvin and Beza that a layman should do this. Koornheert argued that if, as Beza said, God causes sin, then
He is in reality the author of sin. The Bible, he said,
does not teach such a monstrous thing. Koonheert was at-
tracting such a large hearing and arguing so brilliantly
that great fear was awakened lest the whole structure
of Calvinism in the low countries and political stability
itself would be undermined. No minister seemed to be
able to refute him and so Arminius was commissioned
to do so.

Arminius set himself to the task of answering
Koornheert. He began a serious review of predestination from the Bible itself and particularly from the
Book of Romans. He concentrated on chapter 9, the
Calvinists' stronghold of their doctrine. But the deeper
Arminius went in his study of Romans, the more he
became convinced that what Paul was actually teaching
was a refutation of the kind of predestination Beza was
teaching. The Jews believed that they were divinely
predestined to be saved and that nothing could change
this fact. They said God would be unjust to reject any
Jew. Romans was written precisely to show the distinction between God's absolute historical sovereignty and
the conditions of personal salvation. Personal salvation
is always by faith, not by decree. Herein lies the
righteousness of God.[8] Arminius did not abandon his
belief in divine predestination, then or ever, but he saw
biblical predestination in a different light from that
taught by Beza.

Arminius' scholarly mind was now challenged to
explore the subject more thoroughly. He read the
Church Fathers. In a masterpiece of scholarly research
he compiled evidence in an essay showing that no
reputable "Father" had ever taught Beza's views, nor

[8]Cf. *The Works of James Arminius*, trans. Wm. Nichols
(London: Thomas Baker, 1875), III, 527 ff.

had Calvin's double particular predestination ever been officially accepted by the Church. Surprisingly, Augustine himself, not only before the Pelagian controversy but following it as well, taught full moral responsibility. [9] The refutation of Koornheert's "heresy" never materialized.

As a result of his study, Arminius began to preach a series of sermons of exposition from the Roman letter. He did not attack the extreme views of his colleagues but opened the true and rich meaning of Romans to the people. Finally his critics noticed that there was no emphasis on supralapsarianism. Instead of asking him about it openly, they initiated a whispering campaign against him. He had, they said, become a Catholic, a semi-Pelagian, because of his early association with the priest. And didn't his later trip to Rome with a friend reveal his secret Catholic bias? The Catholic emphasis was serious, not so much from a theological point of view, but because Protestantism was fighting both the abuses of the Catholic hierarchial system and its heavy-handed political domination.

Whenever Arminius was given a chance to publicly defend his exposition of Scripture, his sound and quiet scholarship won every argument. No one could refute him on the basis of biblical interpretation. Because no one dared finally to stand against him openly, his enemies took his words out of context and attempted in every way to undercut his influence. Arminius was a man of peace and deplored the brewing trouble in the Church, especially if he himself had become the cause of it. He asked for an official public hearing. This was denied him in his lifetime but the Synod of Dort, after his death, was the answer to his plea. However the occasion was much different from the one he had asked

[9]Cf. *ibid.*, II, 354-74.

for, and the opportunity for free debate was completely denied.

Arminius was eventually placed in the chair of theology at Leyden University, with the full knowledge of his theological position. There he ran afoul of Gomarus' "high Calvinism." Gomarus, the New Testament professor, challenged Arminius on the basis of biblical authority. Arminius refused to subject his biblical interpretation to the creeds. In the heat of the controversy it was stated that "Sacred Scripture ought to be interpreted according to the Confession and Catechism." Though this was an extreme statement it was the position underlying the controversy. Arminius answered on the basis of this meaning.[10]

No one ever charged Arminius with mishandling scripture, but only with failing to use scripture to defend a predetermined position. Arminius insisted that authority rested in the Word of God, not in the opinions of men. It behooves men, then, to find out what the Word of God says. The Church rulers virtually wanted Arminius to quit preaching the Bible as final Authority. They argued that he should make the Calvinistic creed the actual final authority. But that left the question of which creed was authority.

The supralapsarian party wanted every pastor to sign the Statement of Faith yearly in order to maintain his relationship to the Church. This would be a means of assuring conformity and stability to the Church and government. Arminius reminded them that they could not agree as to which creed was the authoritative one. He wanted the Bible to be the only basis of orthodoxy and he underscored his opinion by pressing two penetrating questions: (1) Is the word of man to prevail over the Word of God? and (2) Is a Christian man's

[10]Cf. Caspar Brandt, *The Life of James Arminius*, trans. John Guthrie (London: Ward and Co., 1854), pp. 217-18.

conscience to be bound by God's Word or man's word? The issue was not primarily predestination as such, "but also the role of the magistrate and toleration." There was danger lest the ministry "usurp the power of Christ and thereby develop a new papacy."[11] Theories of predestination were in danger of obliterating the more vital issues festering beneath them.

The full story cannot be told here but we should bring into focus the issues that were involved.

Arminius rejected the supralapsarian concept of God's decrees because:

1. It was not supported by Scripture.

2. It had not been held by responsible Christian scholars in fifteen hundred years and had never been accepted by the whole Church.

3. It made God the author of sin.

4. It made the decree of election refer to uncreated man.

If, as Beza and Gomarus taught, God causes men to sin, then God is the author of sin. Arminius insisted that the supralapsarian logic could not escape this conclusion and he spared no words in denouncing this fallacy.

> Of all blasphemies which can be uttered against God, the most grievous is that by which He is set down as the author of sin; the weight of which imputation is no little aggravated, if it be added that God is on that account the author of sin committed by the creature, in order that He might damn and lead away the creature into eternal destruction, which He had already beforehand destined for him without reference to sin: for so "he would have been the cause of unrighteousness in man, that He might inflict eternal misery upon him." No one will impute such a blasphemy to God, whom everyone conceives of as good. . . . It cannot be imputed to any of the Doctors of the Reformed Churches, that they "professedly set up God as the author of sin." . . . yet

[11]Bangs, *op. cit.*, pp. 5-6.

"it may be that anyone may, from ignorance, teach something from which it may, by fair consequence, be de-
ducted that God is by that doctrine set down as the
author of sin." If this be the case, then . . . [the Doctors]
must be admonished to desert and cast away that doctrine from which the fair inference is drawn.[12]

This would unavoidably make God the only real sinner
in the universe. No one taught such an extreme view,
but Arminius pointed out the fact that a theology determined by logic and not God's Word would ultimately
force this conclusion. Only by grounding theology in
the Word of God could the errors of human judgment
be avoided. Human errors would lead to conclusions
that would destroy the very heart of the Christian
faith.

Arminius died (1609) before the theological problems were brought to a head. His followers carried on
the battle, each in his own way. Some were true to
Arminius' evangelical spirit (Episcopius). Others saw
deeper issues at stake, even such things as separation
of church and state and the roots of democracy (Hugo
Grotius, the "Father of International Law"). Limborch
interpreted the Arminian conflict in a theologically
liberal way and made Arminianism seem to destroy
Christian faith.

We should summarize Arminius' teaching, now, as
it relates to our predestination (holiness) problem. His
principles begin to show how the theories of predestination lead toward or away from the later Wesleyan
doctrine of holiness. Arminius laid the foundation for
a biblical doctrine of holiness, though he himself did not
develop the doctrine.

1. *Arminius' principles regarding predestination:*

a. The doctrine of predestination must be biblical
and not primarily logical or philosophical. (This point

[12]Arminius, *op. cit.,* III, 645-55.

of view would become Wesley's principle later in history.)

    b. Predestination must be understood Christologically. Christ, not the decrees, is the Source and Cause of salvation.

    c. Salvation must be evangelical, that is, by personal faith in Christ.

    d. On the one hand, no theory of predestination is biblical which makes it logically necessary to say that God is the author of sin; yet, on the other hand, it must not be logically possible to say that man can be the author of his own salvation.[13]

    2. *Arminius' predestination theory in terms of four decrees:* [14]

    a. "God decreed to appoint his Son, Jesus Christ . . . who might destroy sin by His own death." Christ is the Elect Man. Individual persons are not chosen to salvation, but it is Christ who has been appointed as the only Saviour of men. *The way of salvation is predestined.* In this way, the whole concept of predestination is changed, (1) from an emphasis on the specific human individual to Christ, and (2) from divine decrees to the conditions of salvation, namely, that Christ is the Saviour and the Door rather than election or divine decrees being the S a v i o u r and Door. "It was [Arminius'] well-grounded fear that Beza and Gomarus, the supralapsarian interpreters of Calvin, were in danger of divorcing the doctrine from Christology and making Christ the mere instrument or means of carrying out a prior, abstract decree. Arminius sought to state the doctrine in the light of Scripture and in integral relation to Christology."[15]

    [13]*Ibid.*, II, 392-93.

    [14]*Ibid.*, I, 247-48.

    [15]Carl Bangs, "Arminius: An Anniversary Report," *Christanity Today,* Oct. 10, 1960, p. 18.

Karl Barth's criticism of Calvinists is that they tend to leave Christ out of their theory of election. Bromiley's analysis of Barth's criticism is, "They begin with the prior decree of God, which really has very little to do with Christ at all; Christ is merely 'dragged in,' as it were, as an agent for the fulfilling of this decree, which is an absolute, unknown decree, according to the Calvinistic interpretation." Bangs notes that there is no mention in this initial statement about man's faith or God's foreknowledge. Rather the whole emphasis is on "the absolute decree, with Christ as its object."[16]

b. God has decreed that those who would repent and believe would be received into God's favor. The major emphasis is on "in Christ." For His sake and through Him, salvation is assured to those who persevere.

c. God has appointed the means (the power) by which to achieve His purpose. Grace was to be given to all men making it possible for any man to turn to Christ and trust in Him. This is prevenient grace, which preserves mankind savable. By this grace men are given the power to believe. But God will not believe for us. The ability is from God, but the act of believing must be man's own act.

d. God predestines on the basis of divine foreknowledge. He knows who will believe and who will not and predestines accordingly. Bangs observes again that to isolate any one of these four statements from the rest and to treat them individually is to miss the whole point Arminius is making. Christ as the elected and only Saviour must be the Foundation of the whole system, with the other three rooted in and deriving their meaning from it.[17]

    [16]"The Debate over Divine Election," *Christianity Today*, Oct. 12, 1959, p. 16.
    [17]*Ibid.*, p. 13.

In the contrast between the Calvinistic and Arminian position on predestination lie the rest of the differences in concepts of sanctification today.

SUMMARY OF THE ARMINIAN VIEWS

Arminius did not reject the fact of predestination or the biblical teaching regarding it, but he showed by careful exegesis that Beza's interpretation of predestination was not biblically sound. The source of the supralapsarian theory of decrees (or any system of decrees which gives specific direction to a theological system) was twofold: (1) It assumed certain things about God and His method of operation about which the Bible gives us no revelation. At this point, human knowledge must always bow in humility before God, but it is at this point where men are often the most dogmatic; (2) The related error was in supposing that (a) God's method of operation was by means of decrees, and (b) that men could know the order in which God arranged them. That which is done in the "eternal secret council of God's own mind" is assumed to be revealed by human intelligence, which then becomes the standard of orthodoxy.

The concept of "particular" predestination naturally suggests the need for decree; else how could God predestine anything? The concept of decree reveals the theologian's concept of God. It is here that Arminius felt Beza's philosophy was defective. Actually, what is a decree? God may or may not order the affairs of the universe by decrees, or at least by man's interpretation of decree. But it is most certainly the case that the Bible does not give us any hint as to the nature or sequence of His decrees; therefore theological differences arising from the various orders of decrees are not proper sources of theological differences and breaks in Christian fellowship.

A more recent Calvinist, Dr. A. A. Hodge, has modified the more extreme concept of divine decrees: "We
believe that the Decree of God is one single, eternal
intention. There cannot be an order of succession in
His purpose. The whole is one choice. . . . The question,
therefore, as to the Order of Decrees is *not* a question
as to the order of acts in God's decreeing, but it *is*
a question as to the true relation sustained by the several parts of the system which he decrees to one another."[18] This makes clear, however, that the relationship
of parts to the whole is a theological problem, not a biblical problem. And the theological systems arising out
of a supralapsarian or sublapsarian concept of the decrees
results in significant and irreconcilable soteriological
contradictions.

The various philosophically determined orders of
God's decrees confuse the truth of the biblical doctrine
of predestination. The biblical doctrine of predestination stands guard against any theory of man's natural
ability intended to defend the absolute sovereignty of
God against Pelagius' teaching that man is not absolutely dependent upon God's grace. God is sovereign. This
truth was shared by the Reformers, Calvin, Beza, Arminius, and later by Wesley.

Calvin's doctrine of predestination stood against the
Catholic error of salvation by the Church,[19] and one's
own good works.[20] This is surely a proper motive.
But when, by the intrusion of man's concept of divine

[18]A. A. Hodge, *Outlines of Theology* (New York: A. C.
Armstrong and Son, 1905), p. 230.

[19]"In common with the earlier Reformers, he [Arminius]
opposed the exclusive claim of the Roman Church by appeal
to the sole authority of Scripture" (Bangs, "Arminius, an Anniversary Report," *Christianity Today*, Oct. 10, 1960, p. 18).

[20]"Calvin and his disciples had used the biblical figures
of election and predestination to express the truth of *sola
gratia* to combat the Roman doctrine of works" (*Ibid.*).

decrees, predestination becomes a speculative doctrine which presumes to know the inner secrets of God's mind, then it no longer serves the interests of Christian theology.

Arminius' teaching was an ethical criticism of the supralapsarian concept of predestination. The implications of this theory tend to relax moral integrity. If God is the author of sin as well as of salvation, why should man attempt to reform his evil ways? The implications inherent in supralapsarianism tend to rob Christianity of its dynamic evangelism as well as high ethical discipline.

Arminius stressed an interpretation of predestination which understood God's grace as strengthening moral life rather than weakening it. Grace is God's love and moral energy available to all men. Grace is not, he thought, an arbitrary imposition of the will of God on passive man. Grace is not an arbitrary divine cause but the free gift of God's enablement.

To Arminius, predestination must be, as it is in Scripture, *Christ-centered*, as all theology must be Christ-centered. This emphasis on Christ was the major corrective of Calvinism's errors and the major Arminian emphasis.

Final authority for Christian faith and theological truth is God's Word. In fact, God's Word must become the judge of the creeds. Therefore theology and the creeds are not to make authoritative proclamations about God's nature and work before thorough exegetical work in the Scriptures is done. Here alone is this kind of revelation to be found. And theology must *always* stand under the judgment of the Word of God.

III *Theological Characteristics of Calvinism, Arminianism and Wesleyanism*

The specific differences in today's evangelical theological world begin to emerge more meaningfully as we proceed with this brief history on the foundation of the preceding historical survey.

After Arminius' death, Simon Episcopius, an able scholar and faithful Christian, picked up and carried on Arminius' unfinished work. He and his friends, called "Remonstrants," formulated the Arminian position in preparation for the public hearing which was to be finally realized. The Synod countered the Arminian points by what is now known as the "Five Points of Calvinism." The following chart shows the contrast between the two points of view:

The Remonstrants' Five Propositions	The Calvinistic Answer
1. *Conditional Election*—on the basis of foreknowledge.	1. *Unconditional Election* or *Particular Predestination.*
2. *Universal Atonement*—limited by man's individual faith.	2. *Limited Atonement*—only for those who are elected.
3. *Natural Inability*—of any man to do good apart from divine grace.	3. *Natural Inability* or *Total Depravity*—regeneration must precede conversion.
4. *Prevenient Grace*—which accounts for all good in mankind. This grace may be resisted and made ineffectual by a sinner's perverse will.	4. *Irresistible Grace* or *Effectual Calling*—the man on whom God bestows grace will be saved; he cannot resist grace.
5. *Conditional Perseverance*—though God provides sufficient grace to meet any possible emergency, men may neglect this provision and fall from grace to eternally perish.	5. *Final Perseverance*—unconditional eternal security.

The Synod of Dort opened November 13, 1618, and continued through 154 sessions, ending May 9, 1619. One hundred two Dutch Orthodox Calvinists were official members of the conference together with 28 delegates from foreign c o u n t r i e s. Thirteen Arminian representatives were present, but they were prisoners of state, condemned for treason because of their views about theology and tolerance in every area of church and state; hence they had no voice or vote. As a result, the Five Points of Calvinism were unanimously declared to be the official Calvinistic position, and the Remonstrants' Five Points heretical.

The Synod defined Calvinism in its infralapsarian form and remains the authoriative statement of "high Calvinism" today. High Calvinism today equates its own views with Christianity as such, saying, "One is not a Calvinist because 'one was brought up in it,' nor because 'it suits one's emotional make-up,' nor because it is 'socially desirable.' One adheres to Calvinism solely because it is the only truth. . . . He who is not with us is against us."[1]

Anything less than the full Five Points is dismissed as being not only "un-Calvinistic" but actually unchristian, theologically speaking.

Arminius lived and died a "Calvinist." Arminius' Arminiamism is not Pelagianism or any degree of it. There are many streams of theology and political ideology called A r m i n i a n that lead far afield from Arminius' teaching. Most of today's C a l v i n i s m is "Arminianized" Calvinism. It is evangelical and evangelistic. But high Calvinism is neither evangelical nor evangelistic. But there are many kinds of Calvinism, some as liberal as Arminian liberalism. Neither "Calvinism" nor "Arminianism" as terms can be used meaningfully without proper definition.

We may now notice the specific theological characteristics of these three main Protestant traditions. It should be remembered first of all that the "ism" fol-

---

[1]Justus M. Van der Kroef, "Calvinism as a Political Principle," *Calvin Forum,* Feb., 1950.

lowing these names may represent quite different teachings from those held by the original persons who gave them their names. Because these great Christian thinkers hammered out their positions in controversy, they tended to be more e x t r e m e than they would otherwise have been. At least, the major point of controversy was often raised to a vulnerable position unguarded by cool and careful scholarship. Followers, too, often select certain emphases from the master's teachings to develop on their own, thereby putting them into different contexts and so altering the meanings somewhat.

With these tendencies in mind, it will be our purpose now to examine briefly those theological traditions which have contributed to contemporary movements, born of an intermingling of them. A useful classification follows:

High Calvinism; Arminianism; Wesleyan Arminianism; mild, low, or modified Calvinism (sometimes called neo-Calvinism); and two interesting mixtures, (a) Wesleyan Calvinism and (b) Calvinistic Wesleyanism, the first disclaiming any essential relation to Wesley or Arminius and the second rejecting any relationship to Calvinism. If this seems confusing, be assured that more confusion exists where some classification such as the above is not recognized and understood.

High Calvinism

So called high or extreme Calvinism is defined by the Five Points of the Synod of Dort and elaborated in the Westminster Confession of Faith. It says that certain men and angels are predestinated by God for the manifestation of His glory to salvation and others to damnation. The number in each case is absolutely set and unchangeable. Those destined to salvation and chosen before creation were elected by God's free will with no obligation of any kind on the part of the one

to be saved. These elect persons' salvation is unconditionally applied and they are assured of all the benefits of the atonement. All others are passed by.[2]

The Five Points are logically consistent. If *God's
absolute sovereignty* is interpreted as Augustine and
Calvin did (the premise), then the rest of the system
follows by logical necessity. No one point can stand
alone. In fact, any deviation at all destroys the whole
system. But if God is *not* like this system presumes
Him to be, perhaps none of the points are true and the
whole system collapses like a house of cards. Everything rests on its distinctive doctrine of God.

Calvinism's concept of God's absolute sovereignty
is interpreted in such a way that any contrary will in
any creature constitutes a threat to this sovereignty.
Therefore, by logical necessity, God's absolute sovereignty makes any genuine human initiative impossible.
Though this concept does not permit any sense of fellowship with God, it does support the sense of stability
which men seek. Calvinists are usually assured that
what they do and what comes to them are directly
from God's hand. Men's actions are not to be accounted for by God's *permissive* will but by God's
governing will. The only freedom is the freedom to
do God's will. God may cause men to sin but God
does not thereby sin. God is under no law but His own
will. God's will is creative and causative, so His will
puts Him under necessity to accomplish that will.
Therefore nothing He does can be called sin because
what He does arises out of His own holy nature. It
follows that the concepts of justice in God and man
have no necessary relationship. God's character is
inscrutable; hence it is not subject to man's judgment
nor is it a pattern for man's concepts of justice, love,
mercy, or any of the virtues.

[2]Cf., Benjamin Warfield, *The Westminster Assembly and Its
Work* (London: Oxford University Press, 1931), pp. 148-50.

William Shedd, a Calvinistic scholar, said, "The doctrine of predestination is too hard for new Christians. Never teach it to babies in Christ. Predestination is for settled, mature Christians only."[3]

In another place Shedd reveals his position relative to the value of the creed over Scripture. Whenever there is a verse of Scripture which says *all men* are under the atonement, he says that this means "all elect men." All those texts which say that Christ died for the whole world mean a particular and select segment of persons spread over the whole world. The scripture which says "whosoever will" or "all who believe" "really means those to whom faith is given."[4]

In this way, an a priori concept of God leads to a principle of biblical interpretation which, in turn, determines the direction of theology and provides an understanding of soteriology.

This "fixed fate" theology is reflected in a lack of evangelistic urgency. Either there is no evangelistic program at all (since to offer an invitation to men would constitute a defiance against God's sovereign will) or the preaching appeal is made with the conviction that *only* the elect and *all* the e l e c t will respond. Such preaching often lacks the gracious, heartbroken, tender, winsome appeal of the preacher who, as Paul, made every kind of personal sacrifice in order to commend himself as Christ's messager to men in order to win them to his Lord (I Cor. 9:16-22). Some high Calvinists refuse to cooperate with Billy Graham because he invites men to Christ, and this makes him an "Arminian." Nothing better illustrates the confusion of mind which ignorance of historical fact engenders.

[3]*Dogmatic Theology* (New York: Charles Scribner's Sons, 1888-94), II. 460.

[4]*Ibid.*, II, 464-70.

Two extreme and theologically opposing streams of theology flow from high Calvinism. One is the "orthodox" stream just described. The other stream flows into the so-called neoorthodox movements. This is not the place to describe this movement except to say that the "orthodoxy" is either Lutheran or Calvinistic. We will simply note two or three significant characteristics. God is the Absolutely Other, the Unapproachable, Unknowable One who predestines every motion of the universe. Theological predestination, however, is not selective but universal. Preaching is not to pursuade men to turn to Christ but to help men to realize that God's forgiveness includes all men. In this view, salvation is conceived in a "beyond history" sense and "universalism" prevails in that mythological framework of thinking.

Many "Calvinisms" lie between the classical and contemporary interpretations. Interpretations of sanctification are consistent in each case with the prevailing philosophy which structures the theological approach.

ARMINIANISM

Enough has been said in this study about Arminius to "locate" him in the theological stream. Arminius himself was evangelical to the core, and his personal insights picked up by Wesley and others have no slightest hint of theological heresy. However, some of Arminius' followers did wander into Pelagian rationalism. In this way Arminius' teaching was perverted and led to theological liberalism which exalted man and denied his need for a Saviour. There is no evangelism in liberalism but for different reasons than that for high Calvinism and neoorthodoxy. In the case of liberal Arminianism (and there the "ism" must serve to distinguish liberalism from Arminius) men are not considered to be so bound in sin that they need to rely upon a Saviour. Education and the correction of social inequalities make it possible to "redeem" men from their predicament. Evangelism, in this context of thought, is a superficial and unrealistic attempt to solve human problems and is dismissed as totally outdated and irrelevant.

Evangelical Arminianism is based on the Remonstrants' Five Points. An evangelical Arminian is one who believes that God, in Christ, extends His love to all men and that each man must accept personal responsibility for his attitude toward that love.

Wesley answered the question, "What is an Arminian?" (in an essay by that name) by saying that Arminians affirm original sin as strongly as the Calvinists and teach justification by faith. They hold that Christ died for all men but that men may resist God's love, and believers *may* make eternal shipwreck of faith. Calvinists believe that predestination is absolute; Arminians believe that salvation is conditioned on faith in Christ. Wesley was sure that many who opposed the Arminians did not understand what they opposed. Wesley was concerned that careful scholarship accompany the Christian minister who sought to interpret theological positions and who used theological "labels."

Basically, Arminianism is an ethical protest against the antinomian tendencies of Calvinism. If men are in every way determined by predestination, the ethical demands of holiness are not relevant to the Christian life.[5]

WESLEYANISM

John Wesley's major contribution to theology was a correction of a popularly held view of faith and a development and projection of this doctrine into every area of theology and the Christian life.

[5]Lowell Atkinson, "The Achievement of Arminius," *Religion in Life*, Summer, 1950, p. 422.

Arminius had released faith from the "prison" of the decrees but it remained for Wesley to take the emancipated "faith" and put it into the very heart of religion. Now Luther's "justification by faith" would have a twin truth, "sanctification by faith." This put a new shade of meaning to faith—an ethical dimension reflected back from the word sanctification.

Wesley's faith was not merely an intellectual affirmation or a superadded gift of God to the elect, but a new way of life, the enthroning of a new Master.

Calvin's emphasis had been on perfection in faith. Wesley taught that full salvation is perfection of love and obedience. One is static; the other is dynamic in that faith issues in faithfulness and works of love. Faith is not the end but the means to the end of restoring man to God's love shed abroad in the heart (see Wesley's sermon "Righteousness of Faith"). "We acknowledge no faith but that which worketh by love" ("An Earnest Appeal"). "Faith becomes the means of which love is the end" ("Law Established Through Faith"). "Being a Christian means having a faith which is active in love" ("Nature of Enthusiasm").

Faith is not the cause of salvation but the condition of receiving it. Our faith does not save us, but we are saved only by Christ, in whom we have faith.

Wesley also maintains that faith cannot be a substitute for sanctification. The doctrine of salvation by faith must not encourage any loss of love and obedience. "The imagination that faith *supercedes* holiness is the marrow of antinomianism."[6]

Good works follow faith but cannot precede it ("Farther Appeal"). There is a tendency on the Continent (western Europe) to dismiss Wesley as a moralist and not worthy of serious theological interest.

[6]Sermon, "On the Wedding Garment," *A Compend of Wesley's Theology* (New York: Abingdon Press, 1944), p. 167.

Though Wesley was concerned about conduct, it cannot properly be said that his theology was obscured or negated by his emphasis on experience if the full meaning of his teaching is allowed to come into focus.

"But is this the faith of assurance, or the faith of adherence?" asks Wesley. He answers that there is no scriptural mention of such a distinction. There are not different kinds of faith, only a difference in degree. "By this faith we are saved, justified, and sanctified; taking that word in its highest sense" (*Sermons*, "The Scripture Way of Salvation"). In other words, whatever faith is, it is that which leads from one point to another in salvation. To cease to exercise faith is tantamount to relinquishing all Christian status. To continue in faith is to be led from the lowest to the highest experiences of grace.

Faith, then, to Wesley was much more than mere belief. The emphasis in faith is not in faith itself, but in the object of one's faith. "Belief in" something is a static concept. It does not necessarily involve any change in action. To have "faith in something" does involve a relationship. For Wesley, faith could not save anyone; but faith in Christ could, because by it Christ becomes the central Object of one's love and obedience.

Faith, then, has an ethical meaning. It means a realignment of life to please God. Faith in God is tremendously important because sin began at the point where faith in Him broke down. A life of sin follows the loss of faith in God because unbelief kills love. Evangelical faith is the foundation for the new love and obedience. And love and obedience are what holiness is. Faith does not make love and obedience unnecessary but, on the contrary, fosters the growth of love and obedience. Christian perfection is the love and obedience which faith in Christ initiates and develops.

John and Charles Wesley lived about a century

after Arminius' death. They were faced by two sources of error in British religion. One stemmed from liberal Arminianism; the other from cold, high Calvinism. Neither of these answered the needs of hungry hearts or was able to arise to challenge the great social evils which were undermining the nation's strength. In answer to these errors the Wesleys raised a strong biblical appeal: (1) The necessity of a personally transforming experience of God's pardoning grace for committed sins, (2) the Holy's Spirit's cleansing power to remove the stain of inbred sin, and (3) a life worthy of God to be lived in this world and which answered the needs of a society shot through with selfishness and greed.

Wesleyan—Arminianism

John Wesley encountered Arminius' writings and was deeply impressed by them. He edited a magazine for many years called the *Arminian,* in which holiness doctrine was proclaimed. Wesley, however, carried Arminius' theological position one step further than Arminius did himself. Arminius held a high view of sanctification but failed to see, as Wesley came to see, that sanctification also is received by faith and is administered by the Holy Spirit. Wesleyanism is Arminian orthodoxy infused with the warmth and power of the Holy Spirit. Arminius saw only dimly what Wesley saw clearly. Both were men of the Word of God and both were dominated by that Word. In this respect they became our proper forebears. Neither man would have tolerated a movement called by his name. Both, in a historically new sense, grounded his theology in the Word of God, not philosophy.

Wesleyan-Arminianism opposes Pelagian liberalism by insisting upon the need for Christ, the Redeemer, who must save us from actual and inbred sin. It also opposes the antinomianism of high Calvinism by the doctrine of deliverance from the "taint of depravity," and the doctrine of grace which enables man to live without willful sin in this life.

Wesley's emphasis was not on free will, as is so often supposed.[7] His emphasis was on free grace, or prevenient grace, granted to any and all men and accounting for all the good found in the world. Natural man is devilish, evil, wholly corrupt. Any good in any man is only by the free grace of God. Man is totally corrupt and helpless in himself. Grace is back of every good or ability in man.[8] Not even the Christian, no matter how established he may be, possesses goodness in himself.

The Christian, Wesley explained, is not like a tree that lives from its own root system. Rather he is a branch "in Christ," which if it is separated from the Tree dies and is destroyed. Christ is our Life and our Righteousness. We must be covered every moment by the atoning blood of the lamb of God.[9] The human person is still human. Yea, more truly human than in his unsaved state. He is weak, ignorant, fallible, temptable. He must always have a fresh supply of God's grace—not to suppress the humanness of man, but to strengthen the inner man by the Holy Spirit.

Wesley added an essential element to the Arminian insight, the work of the Holy Spirit. And this dynamic is what constitutes a new and far-reaching element in today's evangelical theology. The implications of this emphasis will be pointed out in the last section of this study.

[7]Robert E. Chiles in an article entitled "Methodist Apostasy from Free Grace to Free Will" (*Religion in Life,* Vol. XXVII, No. 3, 1958) gives a clear and convincing account of this transition and shows Wesley's true emphasis. See also Wesley's sermon "Free Grace."

[8]Leo George Cox, *John Wesley's Concept of Perfection* (Kansas City: Beacon Hill Press of Kansas City, 1964), pp. 30-31.

[9]John Wesley, a *Plain Account of Christian Perfection* (Kansas City: Beacon Hill Press of Kansas City, 1966), pp. 53-54

IV *Wesleyan Influence on Classical Theology*

Neo-Calvinism (Mild, or Low Calvinism)

Under the biblical impact of Arminius' and Wesley's preaching, the doctrine of "particular" or personal pre-destination began to crumble in most segments of Calvinism. When the emphasis on the doctrine of the Holy Spirit weakened the whole rigid structure of Calvinism, there came a new emphasis on evangelism. In contemporary times such men as Wilbur Smith

(*The Word of God and the Life of Holiness*) and Bernard Ramm (*The Witness of the Spirit*) are infusing the Calvinistic position with the same evangelistic dynamic which inspires Wesleyanism.[1]

We have seen that the doctrine of particular predestination is a necessary logical step toward the conclusion that the elect are unconditionally secure for time and eternity. Unconditional eternal security is the final step in a logical system. It cannot stand alone without the whole system of the decrees to support it.

But, strangely enough, some Calvinists retain only two of the Five Points (and ignore, if not reject, the rest), namely, (1) absolute human depravity and (2) the unconditional eternal security of the believer. The commonly accepted meaning of eternal security is that once a person has trusted in Christ or "accepted Christ" (not a biblical term) he can never be lost no matter what he may do subsequently.

Since we are trying to analyze the theological structure underlying the distinctions between Calvinists and Wesleyans, it is of very great interest to notice that a subtle change has taken place in Calvinism. In the mild Calvinists' view, it is not God's eternal decree which limits and assures salvation but man's own one momentary act of faith which becomes the basis of assurance and security. As a sinner he is free to choose or reject Christ, but as a Christian he loses the power of contrary choice. As a sinner, he is morally responsible to obey; but when he becomes a Christian, God no longer condemns his sin

[1]In a "Debate over Divine Election" reviewed in *Christianity Today* (Oct. 12, 1959), Dr. H. Orton Wiley's answer to the question, "Has Calvinism led to the results predicted by Arminians?" was unchallenged. He said, "What passes for Calvinism, today, is not Calvinism. It is Arminianized. The fact is, Presbyterianism in this country [U.S.] is Arminianized . . . I think few folk today teach Calvinism."

but condones it, closes His eyes to it. Donald Barnhouse declares that not even faithfulness is required
after that one moment of faith which eternally changes
our relationship to God. Obedience is classed as works
and as such is "filthy rags."[2]

George E. Ladd in an article entitled "Justification" said:

> Christ took our hell: nothing is left but heaven. Christ
> paid my debt, God will not collect twice. All our sins,
> past, present and future, are covered. We need not
> fear, we cannot be lost. When a man has received the
> work of Christ upon the Cross and has exercised strong
> faith, for him, *the future judgment has already taken
> place.* . . . This is not restoration to innocence. . . .
> Justification frees us from guilt not only of the years
> before we believed in Christ, but of our entire life up
> to the day of judgment. The man of faith is on the
> heavenward side of the day of judgment. . . . It is
> as though we had already entered heaven.[3]

Barnhouse says again, "When once you have entered into the great truth that God cannot deny himself,
that you are saved and safe in Christ, and that God
himself cannot remove us from Christ, at that moment
true holiness begins."[4] Wesley was particularly concerned about any religious philosophy which stepped
from sin to heaven "without any holiness coming in
between." And yet some mild Calvinism is rooted in
a philosophy which makes this leap from conversion
to heaven not only possible but inevitable.

Calvinist Christians usually live better than their
theology and often put Wesleyan Christians to shame
by their deeply spiritual lives and their fervent, sacrificial, dynamic witness for Christ. But it remains true
that a belief in an evil human nature that cannot be

[2]Donald Gray Barnhouse, "Eight Things God Cannot Do."
Eternity, Jan., 1958, Vol. 9, No. 1, p. 27.

[3]*Eternity*, July, 1958, Vol. 9, p. 12.

[4]*Loc. cit.*

changed in this life coupled with a belief in unconditional eternal security, tends to rob Christians of the spiritual victory which the Bible teaches is possible.

WESLEYAN CALVINISM

Wesley made a most profound impression on religion and on theology. Wesley's emphasis on the work of the Holy Spirit and the evangelistic zeal which accompanied his revivals awakened a hunger in the hearts of Christians everywhere. It has been recognized that the stream of spiritual vitality which flowed from the Wesleyan revivals accounts for the modern missionary movements. Some Calvinism has been profoundly vitalized by the spiritual dynamic of the Wesleyan emphasis.

We have spoken of a Wesleyan Calvinism and a Calvinistic Wesleyanism. There are no movements known by these names, of course, but there are movements bearing these characteristics and in them lie the tensions between holiness and predestination which we need to recognize.

Marriage of Ideas

Calvinism with a Wesleyan emphasis is the result of uniting Calvinism's doctrine of human depravity and unconditional eternal security to Wesley's doctrine of the work of the Holy Spirit. Wesley's teaching relative to victory over sin and dynamic power for service is fused to Calvin's concept of human nature which says that it is antagonistic to grace and cannot be reformed in this life.

This strange, illogical, and unnatural marriage of ideas results in a strange and confusing theology. This theology teaches that human nature cannot be changed in this life, but it can be controlled—not by man himself, but by the Holy Spirit. The believer has the choice of yielding himself (1) to his own base nature or (2) to the Holy Spirit. In this alternative, at least two distinct levels of Christian life are recognized. Both are said to be consistent with Christian status. The Holy Spirit sets up a conflict with "the flesh" or human nature, and this lifelong conflict is the badge, the hallmark, the sign of Christianhood. Inner war is a sort of assurance of the presence of the Holy Spirit.

In this view, human nature is an enemy to be conquered. Every activity and desire of human nature is under suspicion. Every act is tainted by unconscious evil. It would be presumptuous to claim to have a proper motivation, for no man can know himself. The Holy Spirit sits as a slave master over human nature, suppressing its manifestations and exhibiting His power for Christian service, not by using human nature but in spite of human nature.

Calvinism which has been "invaded" by the Wesleyan doctrine of the Holy Spirit, and which we are calling Wesleyan Calvinism, speaks of "surrendering" to the Holy Spirit—of being "possessed by" the Holy Spirit. "Surrender" has a connotation which is not biblical apart from the concept of active stewardship. Biblical surrender is not taking one's hands off but presenting one's hands to God for the fullest measure of active and responsible obedience.

In Wesleyan Calvinism there is little stress usually on the *crisis* of surrender but only on the *attitude* of surrender, which may or may not deepen and mature as life goes on. Surrender is usually stressed only as an aid to victorious life and service. It is not essential to salvation, for nothing can change the eternal security of the believer. "Possessed" is another non-biblical word with danger in it. As it suggests a vacating of the self from the personality, its place to be taken by another Self, the Holy Spirit, the unwholesome nature of the concept can be readily seen.

A more detailed analysis of the Wesleyan Calvinist's view of human nature will be attempted in the last chapter of this study but at this juncture a few key points should help toward an understanding of this position. The Calvinistic view of sinful human nature is basic to the Wesleyan Calvinist. Says Leo George Cox, in *John Wesley's Concept of Perfection:*

> It seems safe to conclude that, from a Reformed point of view, all acts of a sinner are sin, because they proceed from an evil heart, and since the believer still is sinful in nature, all his acts are tainted by sin, so therefore he sins. There does not seem to be any sense in which it can be said that one ceases to sin when he believes.[5]

"God cannot improve human nature," says Barnhouse. To this sinful human nature, the Wesleyan Calvinist adds a serious biblical concept of spiritual victory by virtue of the presence of the indwelling Christ and the work of the Holy Spirit.

The Holy Spirit and Human Nature

The Spirit-filled life is *superimposed* on the ransomed sinner's life. It is a life enacted on our property but it is a life that is somehow external to our true selves. It is a life of victory that pushes our faculties out of the way, with Christ's active obedience being substituted in principle, but not in practice. "The robe of the believer's righteousness has been woven by Christ. The perfect obedience rendered by the Son of Man is placed to the account of those who have faith in him."[6]

Wesleyan Calvinism is able to bridge the gap between sinful human nature and victory in Christ by a concept of human nature which is neither quite Calvinistic nor Wesleyan. It is a concept which has intruded

[5]*Op. cit.,* p. 46.

[6]L. Nelson Bell, "Righteousness," *Christianity Today,* Vol. II, No. 18, June 9, 1958, p. 19.

itself into the Church at various times but has always been rejected by "main line" Christians. It has been the basis of a number of heresies in the Church, Christology being one of them.

The source of this concept is Gnosticism, a mixture of ideologies including elements of Greek philosophy. It probably arose out of a Platonic view of reality. Human nature is thought to be composed of three distinct and independent entities: body, soul, and spirit. Each has a will, a character, a relationship of its own independent of the rest of the person. In this view, the body is considered to be essentially evil and the spirit at least capable of purity. The body is an enemy of the spiritual nature and actually the prison of the spirit. So long as the spirit and body remain together the spirit will be hindered and shackled by the evil body. Only death can deliver the spirit from its sinful prison.

It is of interest to know that this kind of dualism infected the churches to which Paul wrote in the New Testament. We are made especially aware of the ethical problems in this belief in the Thessalonian and Corinthian letters. These Greek Christians were supposing that they could be saved in their spirits but that their bodies could not be delivered from sin. Therefore physical sins were allowed in their lives and among Christians without any conviction for sin. Fornication, the great cultural sin of Greek life, crept into the Christian community because of the philosophy which said that the actions of the body had no relation to the spiritual life. The body could not "infect" the purity of the spirit, and the spirit could not reform the body.

With an understanding of this background problem we may have a better grasp of the inner meaning of such passages as I Thess. 5:23: "I pray God your whole spirit and soul and body be preserved blameless." Paul was not teaching that man is composed of these unrelated elements of personality. He was telling them that God's grace brings purity to the entire human personality. The person is a *unity* and God's grace brings all the powers of the person into a consistent unity around the lordship of Christ. Paul used the language of Greek philosophy to those who were thinking in terms of that philosophy, but his use of the words shattered the pagan philosophy itself.

Paul's philosophy was not pagan but Hebrew. He held the Hebrew view of the unity of personality. When we see this we can understand Paul's major concern relative to the Greek Christians. In I Cor. 6:19, he told them, "Your body is the temple of the Holy Ghost." And in Rom. 12:1, Paul's exhortation, "Present your bodies a living sacrifice," suggests the exalted and spiritually dignified concept he had of the body as the instrument, not the enemy, of the spirit. Paul's emphasis on the sanctity of the body was significant when considered in relationship to the philosophical error of Greek thought.

Calvinistic doctrine holds to the incurable sinfulness of the whole person. Calvinism, as such, has always rejected the tripartite view of human nature. But in the true Calvinistic view salvation is applied to the whole sinful man who is "covered" by the white robes of Christ's righteousness. But in the view we have called Calvinistic Wesleyanism a basic personality conflict is considered normal for the Christian because of the view of personality it holds. The spirit can be saved but the body or nature cannot be. In this way one may speak of and experience victory, yet be undelivered from sin. A more detailed explanation of this view follows in the last chapter in this study.

Calvinistic Wesleyanism

What we are calling Calvinistic Wesleyanism is a tendency within holiness circles to link a Calvinistic

view of human nature to the concept of the "eradication" of the carnal nature. Wesleyan Calvinism stresses
the subjugation of human nature by the Holy Spirit
because the human and the carnal nature are not distinguished from each other. In this view the carnal
nature cannot be "eradicated" because it is the human
nature itself. Calvinistic Wesleyanism, on the other
hand, conceives of a sort of dual human nature—almost two entities or selves. A familiar question is,
"What is the difference between human nature and
carnal nature?" Eradication, then, is the *removal* of
one of the natures, the carnal nature. And hereon
hangs the problem relative to the use of the term
"eradication."

Because of a faulty concept of human nature, the
work of the Holy Spirit is not properly understood.
Wesleyan C a l v i n i s m tends to overemphasize the
growth aspect, or the gradual subduing of the carnal
nature. On the other hand, Calvinistic Wesleyanism
tends to overstress the crisis aspect of sanctification
to the neglect of the growth aspect. Wesley's more
biblical view of human nature enabled him to relate
crisis and process and to keep them together creatively.

Early Wesleyan theologians illustrate what is meant.
Richard Watson emphasized the *growth* aspect of sanctification and led some later Wesleyans to neglect the
crisis aspect. Pope, and Adam Clarke, on the other
hand, stressed the *crisis* aspect of sanctification and
tended to lose the process or growth aspect. In this
latter case there was a failure to distinguish clearly
between the Calvinistic and Wesleyan c o n c e p t s of
original sin. Therefore, when total freedom from sin
was taught as a crisis experience, and the term eradication used to describe it, the danger was in thinking
that human nature itself was somehow made impervious
to sin or that the total susceptibility to sin was "taken
out." There was not enough teaching about the weak-

nesses and fallibility of human nature remaining after sanctification. The place of growth, discipline, process, and the outreach of love as essential to the sanctified life was all but lost.

> The modern holiness movement tends to stress the crisis aspect of sanctification far more than the process of maturation. . . . Two errors are commonly made: (1) When the term "sanctification" is used, the reference is invariably to the crisis aspect of Christian holiness. (2) The concept of progressive sanctification is . . . confined to the pre-crisis period. As a result, entire sanctification has commonly been conceived as a terminal point with disappointing results.[7]

This teaching tends to make introspective Christians. They are u s u a l l y more concerned about preserving their own grace than in living creatively. Holiness is thought to be something we possess. Wesley had strong words for this idea. In his *Plain Account,* he emphasized the need for a moment-by-moment reliance on the cleansing blood of Christ. No holiness resides in a man apart from the presence of Christ. And there is no holiness which does not issue in love and good works. The holiness that is so obsessed by an examination of one's own emotional states that it has no energy left for self-forgetting Christian service is, to Wesley, not real holiness.

"Crisis" and "experience" are terms which, when properly used and understood, are exceedingly important to Wesleyan theology. It was precisely this practical relating of the truths of theology to human life which distinguished Wesley's contribution to religion. But there are two important points to note.

The first is that *Wesley's spiritual and ethical*

[7]Hollis F. Abbott, "Christian Maturity," in *The Word and the Doctrine,* Kenneth Geiger, ed. (Kansas City: Beacon Hill Press of Kansas City, 1965), p. 301.

emphasis rests on solid theology. Failure to observe this
(1) has resulted in an almost contemptuous neglect
of Wesley in European theological circles. (It is said
that he had no intellectual content—that he was concerned with only superficial and irrelevant moralisms.)
And (2) in America there has been a tendency to select out of Wesley's works only his emphasis on experience, much to the theological impoverishment of
the Wesleyan movement.

The second important point to notice is that *the
essential meanings of crisis and experience can evapo-
rate if and when they are confused with mere psychological reactions.* There is great danger in equating emotion
with experience and/or a specific reaction with
crisis. Even "crisis," when it is limited in meaning to
a time point, many divert attention away from its
crucial and basic meaning, that of a total and permanent
change of direction resulting from a judgment/decision
act. Religious feeling comes over the same psychological
"track" as other feelings. "Crisis" is essentially a total
life commitment, with or without emotion. "Experience" buries this commitment deep into the center of
the self, from which the issues of life arise.

In Calvanistic Wesleyanism there is an overemphasis on special "experience." If there has been a failure
in Christian victory, the tendency is to seek another
"experience" which will make temptation impossible.
"Experience," as valid as this is in Christian life, is
substituted for the equally valid "walk of obedience,"
growth in grace, and all the other aspects of a growing,
disciplined human life in Christ. So great a concern
is held for the subjective experience that little or no
energy is left for dynamic evangelism and missionary
outreach. Congregations believing this way are usually
small, isolated from the spiritual needs of their com-
munities, sometimes of their own homes, and they are
often overly critical of external forms of worldliness

in dress and recreation. They too easily forget that love of neighbor is as essential as total love for God.

Certainly neither Calvin nor Wesley should be blamed for this abnormal situation. But this is another result of attempting to unite the truths of Calvinism and of Wesleyanism without a thorough understanding of the deep meaning of each.

Calvin was e x t r e m e l y interested in the social outreach of the gospel, though he did not relate it to holiness in a theological sense. And Wesley's deepest concern was for the outreach of love, which he related essentially to holiness. Holiness that withdrew from life was to Wesley, not biblical holiness. Love could not be divorced from holiness because love to God and man was precisely what holiness is. Holiness must issue in the fruits of the Spirit.

Summary

We have spoken of theological provincialism. We are using this term to mean any partial truth raised to the status of a whole truth, or any overemphasis of one segment of theology to the neglect of other emphases. When a philosophical concept of God's sovereignty becomes the foundation for a logically bound theological system in which human responsibility is limited beyond biblical teaching and ethical soundness, this is provincial. Conversely, when humanism becomes the premise of a system which divorces man from the absolute need of divine grace, an equally s e r i o u s theological provincialism results.

Any system of human thought limited to strict logic will lead to intellectual provincialisms because logic is necessarily selective. Because of this, unbiblical concepts of predestination and holiness are mutually exclusive. We say "unbiblical concepts" because "biblical concepts" include both of these, and in a truly biblical theology both must be taken fully into account.

DOCTRINAL DIFFERENCES IN THE LIGHT OF BIBLICAL INTERPRETATION

The theoretical problems which have been discussed have very practical consequences. It may be that the theoretical aspect of our religious differences has not seemed important. It may be that we think we are not involved in the theoretical differences which seem to be important to others. But the fact remains that where we do not share an understanding in practical religion we will usually find that we have been unaware of the nature of our basic philosophies and the importance of that of which we have been unaware, namely, our basic presuppositions.

The Doctrine of God and Human Responsibility

Two fundamental questions stand out clearly. These questions lie at the point where theories of predestination and holiness cross. One is a *theoretical* problem which asks how much moral responsibility men may possess without threatening the absolute sovereignty of God. This concern is right. If God's sovereignty is undermined, the whole structure of Christian faith collapses. Therefore whatever logical conclusions may stem from the doctrine of God's absolute sovereignty must be accepted without hesitation, regret, or compromise. God's absoluteness must be preserved at whatever cost to man's moral autonomy.

The second question is *practical*. With how much moral responsibility did a sovereign God endow the men He created? To what degree are men responsible? This turns our attention from speculative concerns to very practical ones. There are three facts to consider:

The *first* fact is a personal matter. All men know themselves to be morally responsible. There are real, not merely fictional, choices to make which are demanded by conscience and from which stem consequences of vital moral reality. The very existence of intelligence testifies to the power of choice and the exercise of it. Take away moral responsibility and personality chaos results.

The *second* fact is a social matter. There is the cold, hard fact that unless men exercise moral control over themselves and their society human existence is debased and its continuance threatened. All the intelligent relationships of men rest on the assumption that men are morally responsible. Punishment for the infringement of human law is based on this assumption. Practical judgments about men—good, bad, honest, careless, weak, indifferent, noble, etc.—are based on this assumption. Take away moral responsibility and social chaos results. There is a moral structure which the rankest libertine assumes. This is not a standard he wishes to apply to himself but a standard which he demands of others. Any philosophy which excuses men from full, mature, moral responsibility destroys itself and those who espouse it. The task of the philosopher is to account for, justify, and clarify this fact of moral freedom and its necessity to maturity.

The *third* fact regarding moral responsibility faces everyone whenever he reads his Bible. The Bible everywhere seems to assume that men are capable of right choices and obligated to make them. No scripture gives any man the slightest excuse for sin. The Bible seems to know that men are sinful, weak, ignorant, rebellious, evil. But it always speaks of God's grace which makes that sin unnecessary. Where sin abounds grace always much more abounds (Rom. 5:20). The Bible condemns *all* sin unqualifiedly. There are no double standards permitted, nor any theories of redemption which leave men in sin while God considers them free from sin. The Bible knows of no "two-nature theory" which condones a sinful nature living in the same "self" with the human nature. Take away the moral responsibility of men and the Bible is an intellectual shambles. The task for the theologian is to account for this and make the necessary theological adjustments.

We have noted that the above problems arise out of some combination of two contrasting ways of explaining God. One view says that God's sovereign will cannot tolerate a contrary will in His universe. To do so would destroy the meaning of sovereignty. The other observes that a sovereign God *does* maintain His sovereignty in company with other wills. Certainly the answer to this dilemma can never be found in philosophy as such. Certainly we, as Christians, should check the accuracy of our assumptions by the Word of God.

Human Presuppositions

This raises another question. Can we read the Bible objectively? None of us is intellectually neutral. We are committed. Our personal prejudices can and do blind us to truth. We tend to find in the Bible, or in nature anywhere, about what we want to find. Our own fixed point of view "filters out" some of the truths we hear. In fact, our prejudices become the "filter" and hence the judge of truth. Or, to change the figure, the shadow of our own provincialism falls on the truth and we interpret the material according to the p a t t e r n formed by our prejudices.

This would present an impossible barrier to truth were it not for the fact that the mind is not a passive thing imprisoned and immobilized by its structure. The mind of man is dynamic—growing, expanding, adjusting, discriminating, relegating, creating. When this fluid "self" permits itself to be arrested at any point in its expanding life so that it no longer accepts new truth, or entertains questions about its past experience, personality breakdown begins. The whole of modern science is a testimony to the ability of the human mind to be self-critical and to be capable of surmounting the chains of prejudice.

Can we read the Bible objectively? We should be ashamed to admit it if we cannot. The Bible was given precisely to challenge and criticize and correct defective human prejudice regarding spiritual and moral matters. Some of us find only God's sovereignty in Scripture, some only man's "freedom." Some find predestination only, others sanctification. The fact is, all of these things are there.

 The Bible never gives us easy, logical pat answers to the huge questions of life, because life is not easy or simple. God is too great to be confined in neat "packaged" theological statements. God is bigger than man's logic and we must include *all* that the Bible says about Him in our theologies. The Bible is revelation. It will never *defend* a theology. It will always stand as a Judge over our theologies to disturb us when we become too sure of ourselves, to correct us, and to instruct us in the truths relative to God and our relationship to Him.

A scientist can become a master of the natural world only as he forsakes his childish and prejudiced opinions about nature and humbles himself enough to become a learner. Nature will remain hidden from the scientist who refuses to be taught by nature. Nature is first, and always, the master to be served before it will submit itself to the scientist's will. The same principle holds for theology and the Scriptures. All of us, Calvinist and Wesleyan, must distinguish carefully and honestly between the Word of God and the opinions and interpretations with which we approach it.

The Bible and Human Experience

One of the major problems in theology is the tendency to oversimplify and "over-abstractize" Christian truth—to reduce Christian truth to neat, consistent, logical statements. In doing so we build a gulf between

theology and the rich and varied truth so necessary
for the complex lives we must live. The Bible was
given *in the midst* of human experience. The Bible
must not be taken away from life.

Calvin's logic satisfies the mind but not the heart,
because life as a whole is greater than logical systems.
Soren Kierkegaard injected a shocking corrective into
theology by pointing out the fact that there is a proper
tension between concept and conduct. Wesley was
conscious of this problem. He cared more about being
soundly biblical than merely logical, though Wesley was
a most rational thinker. For instance, to Wesley, love
which puts men into the center of life relationships
and problems gave meaning to the detachment from the
world and sin which becoming a Christian demanded.
Love itself cannot be truly love unless it also hates evil
and rejects it. But hating sin without the compensation
of love to God and man created a moral vacuum which
would destroy spiritual life. Holiness, to Wesley, was
not abstract but exceedingly practical. Christian perfection *is* consistent with human finiteness and frailty.

These examples of the complexity of truth should
help us to approach the differences between Christian
traditions with a mature and sympathetic spirit. We
have outlined the differences *in principle* between the
theologies relevant to our study of holiness. In the
remaining part of this study it would seem profitable to
lift out several specific doctrines which separate us and
examine them critically and biblically.

There is a cluster of related doctrines around which
tension exists between Calvinists and Wesleyans. These
are: God's sovereignty versus man's freedom; God's
will and God's grace; man's sin and God's grace; salvation by divine decree or by faith; the work of the
Holy Spirit; and eternal security and Christian assurance.

V Theological Tensions Raised by the Doctrine of Particular Predestination

GOD'S WILL AND MAN'S WILL

The most obvious tension raised by Calvinistic predestination is that between God's will and man's will. Is man morally responsible? If he is, how can it be truly said that God is absolutely sovereign?

This is not an academic question only. It is a very real question. The nature of God is involved. God's total sovereignty is the basis of the whole of Christian theology. No philosophical theory which permits the slightest break in that sovereignty can be permitted. Every Christian doctrine hangs on this doctrine. Even the doctrine of man's moral freedom is actually meaningless apart from God's sovereignty. A less than sovereign God cannot support Christian faith.

On the other hand, as we have seen, to deny in any sense the full moral responsibility of man raises serious problems in reference to Christian faith. We have seen that particular predestination is both the *outcome* of a theory regarding God's sovereignty and a *defense* of that doctrine. On the one hand, as the guardian of the nature of God against the unholy pretense of the Roman church in assuming the prerogatives of God, Luther and Calvin raised the doctrine of particular predestination. On the other hand, the same doctrine of predestination became the principle of biblical interpretation. Within the framework of this circular reasoning, the Bible cannot speak for itself. It is known what it must say, or mean, before the Book is opened.

The Augustinian concept of God's absolute sovereignty raises a tension in soteriology. If God predestines particular persons to be saved, what shall we do with the multitude of scriptures that seem to invite *all* men to the fountain of salvation?

Dr. H. Orton Wiley was invited to a "dialogue" between several scholars representing various Calvinistic positions with himself presenting the Wesleyan-Arminian viewpoint. In the course of the discussion Dr. Wiley asked the above question and quoted quite a number of the scriptures referred to. The answer was, "We interpret these passages as good Calvinists."[1]

As a "good Calvinist," Dr. William Shedd explains

[1]"Debate over Divine Election," *Christianity Today,* Oct. 12, 1959, p. 3.

this interpretation in his *Dogmatic Theology.* By a study of the English preposition "for" as it was used in seventeen-century England, and by sharply distinguishing between atonement and redemption, he can say that "Christ died for all men" in the sense of the *intrinsic value* of His act but not in the *intention* of His act. Christ's death was infinitely sufficient for the redemption of any and all men, but the application of redemption is limited to elect men.[2] In other words "whosoever" is addressed to elect men only. In its *extent* Christ's atonement is unlimited; in its *application or intent,* it is limited.

The "mild" Calvinist, such as Henry Theissen, takes the biblical invitations seriously, attributing the election of certain men to salvation to the foreknowledge of God.

Sanctification and a Doctrine of God

Our concept of sanctification as it relates to redemption will be largely determined by our concept of God and His intention in respect of redemption. If God saves us only because of His selective will and a man cannot fail to be saved if it is God's intention to save him, sanctification is either the inevitable outcome of election or it is something reserved for the elected man to obtain after death. If man's moral responsibility is genuinely respected, then sanctification is a matter of prime concern to a Christian. So much rests on our prior concept of God.

Wesley was well aware of this problem. He wrote a particularly virile essay on "Thoughts About God's Sovereignty."[3] First Wesley reminds us that our concept of God, being basic to our whole theology, must be

[2]*Op. cit.,* II, 464-70.
[3]The following quotations are from this sermon as found in his *Works,* V, 361-63.

derived from Scripture, not from philosophy. In his opinion, the predestination error arose from a defective view of God, a one-sided view of God, or in a false emphasis, namely, in God's sovereign will only. God has revealed himself, Wesley says, under a twofold character, as a Creator and as a Governor. These are different but in no way inconsistent. He says:

> You will never speak of the sovereignty of God but in connection with the other attributes: for the Scriptures no where speak of this single attribute, as separate from the rest. Much less does it speak of the sovereignty of God as singly disposing the eternal estates of men. No, no, in this awful work, God proceeds according to the known rules of his justice and mercy.

The sovereignty of God is never to supersede His justice, said Wesley. As Creator, God has acted according to His own sovereign will. Justice cannot be considered in creation. God began creation in His time. "He determined the duration of the universe," the "number of stars," the animate and inanimate "furniture" of the earth, the nature of man, the "time and situation of the birth of every person, the degree of health of every one, the culture in which one would be born." (Few of us would follow Wesley here, as far as he was willing to go with Calvin!)

But "we must absolutely maintain," says Wesley, "that God is a rewarder of them that seek him." He does not reward the sun for shining, nor could He reward us for letting our light shine if we acted as necessarily as the sun.

Wesley comments further that whenever God acts as Governor, or Rewarder, He is not acting as Creator. If God is the Judge of men He must act in justice, not as Sovereign over subjects unable to act freely. "He will punish no man for doing anything which he could not possibly avoid." By holding these two characteristics in balance, Creator and Governor, "we give God the full glory of his sovereign grace, without impeaching his inviolable justice." Whatever we may think of Wesley's scientific theories, his central insight regarding the distinction between the creatorship and governorship of God is valid and helpful.

A Suggested Solution

When a problem is encountered relative to God's sovereignty and man's will, it probably lies in thinking of man's will as standing over against God's will, challenging and defying God so as to constitute a threat to God's will and purpose in His creation. No evangelical Christian would tolerate such an idea. And yet both the full measure of God's sovereignty and a genuine moral responsibility in man must be accounted for and included in one system without absurd reasoning to explain it. May we try to suggest a solution by means of a chart?

The unsatisfactory concept of man's freedom in relation to God's sovereignty could be likened to a set of balancing scales with the weights set against each other.

In this view, God's will is thwarted by man's will or man's will is thwarted by God's will. In either case, one of the two is victor, the other vanquished.

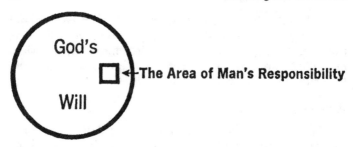

It seems to be more in keeping with biblical teaching to illustrate the proper relationship by a large circle typifying God's sovereign will. The small square contained within the circle is the real though limited freedom which God has given to the man He created. In God's sovereign love He has created morally responsible beings. But man's freedom is strictly limited by God. God makes the rules. Man is genuinely free within the limits set by God. Man lives in an environment where God is Master. God controls nature, the universe, the major lines of history. The natural order is absolute (God is Creator). But there is a vastly different kind of order back of the natural order, namely, the moral order—and the rules are moral rules. God has given men the power of discrimination and the ability to make decisions between alternatives. God's will and mercy sustain moral freedom in man. In fact, God has made man in such a way that he is under constant necessity of making such decisions. He is not free *not* to make constant moral decisions.

But the choices man is compelled to make are not irresponsible. His is a moral, not immoral freedom. Man cannot choose evil and reap good, nor can he make his own rules for the moral life. He cannot dictate the terms of his own salvation. He must choose which bondage (or consequences) he will accept. L u t h e r shocked his hearers by his famous maxim, "The Christian man is the most free man of all and subject to none. But the Christian man is the most bound man of all and subject to all." Joshua cried, "Choose you this day whom ye will serve" (Josh. 24:15). Jesus declared that "no man can serve two masters" (Matt. 6:24). Paul wrote, "Know ye not, that to whom ye yield yourselves servants to obey, his servants ye are . . . whether of sin unto death, or of obedience unto righteousness?" (Rom. 6:16) All this defines the limits of man's freedom, and reveals the divine rules which govern that freedom. Men are free to choose their bondage—but *not* free to choose the consequences.

Hardening of the Heart

According to God's rules, a choice for God leads to certain consequences in the life of the individual— a growth in spirituality and fellowship and sensitiveness to the Holy Spirit. But a choice to disobey God inevitably dulls the sensitivity to the Spirit's ministry, and "hardness of heart" results. When we are told that God hardened men's hearts, reference is made to the moral order instituted by God himself. God does not break the moral rules He has established.

There is a distinct difference between a heart hardened against God in respect to personal salvation and one hardened by God in order to accomplish a specific course in history. When this distinction is carefully made, many problems in interpretation disappear. Pharaoh's heart was not divinely hardened against God so far as salvation is concerned, but in order to bring about a certain event in the salvation history of Israel.

It should also be noted that not all references to God's choice and election have to do with personal salvation. Calvinstic scholars neglect to make this important distinction. Dr. Nicole, in the "Debate over Divine Election,"[4] quotes John 15:16, "Ye have not

[4]*Op. cit.,* p. 15.

chosen me, but I have chosen you, and ordained you."
He significantly ends the quotation at this point. The
following words clearly specify that the choice has to
do with a quality of Christian service which is to be
characteristic of the disciples' work after the Holy Spirit
comes. Dr. Nicole then refers to Romans 9—11, relating what he calls "the priority of the election to the
commission of any particular act" to election to salvation. Arminius showed with exquisite care and
scholarship that this interpretation could not be sustained.

Great care must be exercised in biblical exegesis
to avoid theologizing a passage improperly or reading
theology into a passage where it is not intended. If
this advice were heeded, many theological provincialisms would disappear and theology would profit in all
our denominational traditions.

GOD'S WILL AND GOD'S GRACE

A tension is raised by the concept of God as absolutely sovereign in the light of the biblical concept
of grace. A biblically uncriticized concept of God's
sovereignty leads to the idea of a God who is under
bondage to His own will. What He wills must come
to pass. The definition of grace must fall inside this
framework of thought. Grace, then, can only be God's
power bringing His will to pass.

The consequence of this position is a view of human
personality which lies below the basic minimum demanded by rationality and moral integrity as well as the
demands of the biblical expectation of man so far as
its requirements in relation to him are concerned.

Augustine's Position on Grace

Augustine's teaching expresses this meaning of
grace very well. He reasoned that, if God desired all

men to be saved, none could be lost; therefore grace is the selective power of divine will, since not all men are saved.

This concept inevitably pits one attribute of God against another. For instance, God's grace must clash with His love. His love extends to all creation but His grace selects and thus limits the object of His love.

William Shedd argues that election does not spring out of divine love (*agape*) spoken of in John 14:23 but out of divine goodness and kindness (*chrestoteta* and *aptomian*) spoken of in Rom. 11:22. This bifurcation in God's nature leads Shedd to say, in answer to the objection that the sincerity of God is impugned by a universal offer of salvation to any whom He will not save, that

> 1. God, by reason of His inherent compassion may sincerely desire the conversion of a sinner . . . though He knows it will never take place . . . as a parent desires the reformation of a child, but cannot achieve it. . . .
>
> 2. The decree of God is not always the expression of His desire, but sometimes is contrary to it. God decreed sin, yet prohibited it.[5]

There is one class of scriptures, says Shedd, which teaches that the benevolent desire of God is that all men should turn from sin. Another class teaches that, for reasons unknown to man but sufficient to God, God determines in some instances not to gratify His own desire. There is nothing self-contradictory in this, Shedd argues, because a parallel situation is found in human action.[6] God does not ever try to prevent a man from turning to Him but actually helps him by "common grace." Both the elect and non-elect resist God's grace, but "in the instance of election God follows

[5]*Op. cit.*, II, 451-52.
[6]*Ibid.*, p. 453.

up the common grace, which has been rejected, with regenerating grace which overcomes the resistance."[7]

Common Grace

The doctrine of "common grace" was formulated by Abraham Kuyper in the nineteenth century to complete the logic of such characteristically Calvinistic doctrines as divine sovereignty and election, total depravity, and the like. The Christian Reformed church adopted this concept under Three Points: (1) God is kindly disposed to all men; (2) God restrains sin in individuals and society; (3) The unregenerate are capable of civic righteousness. So many problems attend this doctrine that theologians debate the issues endlessly. An interesting "dialogue" is under way between the interpretations of Cornelius Van Til's *Common Grace* and James Daan's *A Theology of Grace,* concerning the nature of grace.

Wesley's View of Grace

Wesley believed the Bible taught another meaning of grace stemming out of another concept of God. In some contrast to Calvinism which emphasized the majestic *power* of God (He creates and redeems because He can do so and wills to do so), and Arminius, who emphasized the *justice* of God (He is not only good but He is fair to all men), Wesley emphasized the *love* of God which takes up and unifies all the attributes of God into a total personality. God's acts do not arise out of His creative will or out of an inner necessity of any kind, but out of His love. God's grace is God's love in action. Grace is the expression of God's moral freedom.

Grace is the majestic expression of God's great love. Creation is the revelation of God's love; hence it is grace. Grace accounts for all that man is. Man, even

[7]*Ibid.*, p. 432.

fresh from God's hand, has no natural ability apart from the immediate application of God's grace. It was "free grace" that "formed man out of the dust of the ground," made him in God's image, and gave him the power of dominion. The same "free grace" continues to sustain us in life and whatever human powers and goodness may yet be ours.

We have previously noted that Wesley did not teach "free will" in man but "free grace" in God. Grace is Christocentric—an outpouring of God's personal nature through Christ. *It is intensely personal;* hence there can be no distinctions in grace such as "common" and "saving grace." Wiley stated the case succinctly in the "Debate over Divine Election": "We hold there is no distinction in the nature of grace between prevenient grace and saving grace, that it's all of one nature. Consequently, we don't draw the distinction frequently drawn in Calvinism, between common and saving grace. We think one merges into the other."[8]

By the same logic, it should be noted, there can be no distinction in grace between justification and sanctification. Not all holiness teachers are alert to this point. This does not mean that there is no distinction between justification and sanctification, but it does relate the two in a way that is not always done. No holiness preacher or teacher can justifiably reject the Calvinists' distinction between common and saving grace who himself makes a distinction between "saving grace" and "sanctifying grace." Certainly the Bible makes no such distinctions.

Since love and grace are q u a l i t i e s of God's personality, the outflow of these qualities is the outflow of God himself. There are not different kinds of grace accomplishing different kinds of results. Rather there are varying kinds of appropriations on man's

[8]*Op. cit.,* p. 4.

part of the benefits of grace. This would account for the differences in Christian experience. Grace is not an impersonal *power*, or a *thing* to be received. It is God making himself available to us. It is the full measure of His redemptive love held out to us without reserve. But the results of grace in man are limited to man's grasp of God. Each step toward God and each step within the circle of His love requires the highest and noblest response of which man is capable at any given time. These are stages on man's way, not different "gifts" on God's part.

God's Grace and Man's Sin

At this point the tension between Calvinism and Wesleyan Arminianism comes to a high point. Without the background understanding of how each tradition has come to its position, our discussion would descend to the level of mutual recrimination. We should now be able to compare the two views with a good understanding of why the differences exist.

That man was made in God's image all Christians agree. However, in Calvinism the image is thought to be totally destroyed, making man wholly and irrevocably corrupt in this life and incapable of any act or word or thought untainted by that corruption. Sin has gone so deep into human nature that it cannot be eradicated in sinner or saint. Grace covers sin but cannot cure it.

To Wesley and those who follow in his train, the image of God is marred in every part but not destroyed, because to destroy the "image" would rob men of humanhood. But, in Wesley's view, the only reason any semblance of humanhood is preserved is by the free grace of God. Without grace men would "bear the image of the devil."

In Calvinism, man's will is moved by grace prior to man's consciousness of it and apart from his awareness of it. Regeneration precedes all faith and

obedience and is applied to the elect only. In Wesleyanism, "grace, or the love of God, whence cometh our
salvation, is free in all, and free for all" (Sermon, "Free
Grace"). Saving grace begins with prevenient grace
extended to all men. No man is found in the "state
of nature." Conscience itself is of grace. "No man sins
because he has not grace, but because he does not use
the grace he has" (Sermon, "Working Out Our Own
Salvation"). The heathen have a measure of grace.
The power to resist grace is of grace. The power not to
sin is of grace. "Holiness begins before justification and
regeneration by the power of grace" (*Ibid.*).

All men come in under the cover of God's free
grace. Christ died for *all* men (Luke 19:10; Matt.
18:14; John 3:16-17; II Cor. 5:14-15; I Tim. 4:2, 6;
I John 2:2; 4:4; Heb. 2:9). It is true that the Wesleyan
and the Calvinist interpret these passages differently;
the former's basic philosophy permitting him to take
these biblical statements at face value; the latter, for
the same reason, being under obligation to a predetermined exegesis. In the "Debate over Divine Election"
already referred to, Dr. Wiley quoted many passages
like the above. Dr. Henry asked, "On what general
principles do Calvinists reply?" Dr. Nicole answered,
"Some of these verses indicate only the fulfillment of
certain conditions. . . . People who actually fulfill these
conditions . . . have been led by God's specific grace,
which in this case [is] elective grace." In defense of
his interpretation Dr. Nicole said, simply, "I accept
wholeheartedly the position of Calvin."[9]

The Image of God

Perhaps a more sound exegesis and exposition could
be made of the whole matter of man's ability to cooperate with God's grace were we to make the distinction

[9]*Ibid.,* p. 16.

so carefully made in Scripture between "God's image
in man" and "man made in God's image."

It is helpful to notice that the Scriptures con-
sistently refer to the "image of God," not as something
in man, but a pattern in which he is made. Man is
what he is because of the way he is made. Were he
to forfeit any part of himself, he would no longer be a
man.

"Created in the image of God," Wiley says, "we
may say then, that man was endowed with certain powers known as the natural image . . . [which is] uneffaced
and ineffaceable, and exists in every human being."[10]
"This natural likeness to God is inalienable. . . . This
first element of the divine image man can never lose
until he ceases to be a man. St. Bernard well said
that it could not be burned out, even, in hell."[11]

The New Testament helps to clear up the abstrac-
tions relative to the meaning of the term "image of
God." We are told that Christ *is* "the image of God"
(II Cor. 4:4; Col. 1:15; Heb. 1:3). We may conclude,
then, that Christ tells us something about ourselves
that we could not otherwise know. G. C a m p b e l l
Morgan says, "[Jesus'] persistent use of the title, Son
of man, for himself, marks His identification with
humanity, and suggests the truth that the final understanding of human nature must result from a knowledge
of himself."[12] The image in which we are made is
precisely Christ. Looking to Him, we see not only our
potential spirituality but our responsibility to God for
that potential.

This being true, we are prepared for the distinction
Wesley makes between man patterned after God in

[10]*Christian Theology*, II, 32.

[11]Augustus Strong, *Systematic Theology* (Philadelphia:
Griffith and Roland Press, 1907), II, 515.

[12]*The Teachings of Christ* (Grand Rapids: Fleming H.
Revell Co., 1913), p. 113.

his *natural* image (a spiritual nature corresponding to God's), man patterned after God in his *political* image (capacity for governorship), and, c h i e f l y, man patterned after God in his *moral* image ("righteousness and true holiness," Eph. 4:24). (Cf. his sermon "On the Fall of Man.")

It is with this in mind that Wiley defines the moral image, not as a possession, but as the use man makes of the powers with which he was endowed at creation. This gives meaning to Rom. 8:29; II Cor. 3:18; and Col. 3:10, where man's approximation to the image of Christ is related (1) to predestination (the way of salvation is predestined); (2) to dedication to the Lord ("changed into the same image from glory to glory"); and (3) to the "new man" which we are to put on. Human but God-given powers, once used to destroy the self, are now used so that "Christ be formed in" us (Gal. 4:19).

If nothing of the essential humanness of man is ever lost and all of these essential powers are evidence of the Christ-pattern in which we are made, then we must conclude that, however low in sin we have permitted ourselves to fall, the moral obligation to use our powers to return to and obey God is imperious. It means that sin does not belong to human nature. It is alien and a leech. That which prevents our "conformation" into His image can and must be relinquished. Furthermore, it can be relinquished by the grace of God.

If, Wesley asks, we are not saved from our sin by God's grace, then what is it that we are saved from? Why did Christ die?

SALVATION BY DECREE OR BY FAITH?

One of the greatest tensions between Calvinism and Wesleyanism is in the meaning of faith as expressed in the Reformation dictum that "salvation is

by faith alone." Herein lies the crux of the difference
between predestination and the doctrine of sanctification. The companion doctrine, "by grace alone,"
actually sets up the tension. If salvation is by grace
alone, then it cannot be by faith alone. But this basic
tension is hidden under the cover of particular predestination or election. The divine decree makes grace
the cause of faith, but in so doing raises the question,
What is evangelical faith? The Calvinist interprets the
Wesleyan concept of faith as a form of works. The
Wesleyan interprets the Calvinistic concept of faith by
elective grace as missing the scriptural concept of moral
responsibility.

These confusions became so entangling that, when
Wesley rejected salvation by election or decree, he
was charged, even by his friends with preaching
salvation by works. In the minds of many people the
divine decree had virtually been made a substitute for
salvation by faith and grace. Wesley's clear mind was
puzzled about this matter until, as he says, "a thought
shot across my mind, which solved the matter at once.
'This is the key: those who hold, "Everyone is absolutely predestined either to salvation or damnation," see no
medium between salvation by works and salvation by
absolute decrees.' It follows, that whosoever denies salvation by absolute decrees . . . asserts salvation by
works."[13] Salvation by decree (predestination), then,
is actually contrary to salvation by faith and the defect
in Calvinism's concept of faith is revealed.

To the objection that faith, separated from the
conditions of predestination, is a form of works, Wiley
answers in Adam Clarke's words:

> Is not faith the gift of God? Yes, as to the grace by
> which it is produced; but the grace or power to believe,
> and the act of believing are two different things. Without

[13]*Works*, VI, 48.

the grace or power to believe, no man ever did or can believe; but with that power the act of faith is a man's own. God never believes for any man any more than he repents for him. . . . *The power to believe may be present long before it is exercised, else why the solemn warnings with which we meet everywhere in the word of God, and threatenings against those who do not believe? Is not this the proof that such persons have the power but do not use it?*[14] (Italics mine)

Wiley continues: "The law of God is written in our minds and in our hearts—in our minds that we may know it, and in our hearts that we may love it. It is the conjoining of these two that makes possible a true obedience of faith."[15]

Wesley stood firmly on the Reformation and biblical doctrine of salvation by faith. Faith makes salvation by decree or salvation by works impossible. But biblical faith, according to Wesley, must work by love.[16] Right here we find the vital distinction between the Calvinistic and Wesleyan concepts of salvation. Calvinism's faith has no essential element of love in it. Wesley's faith (and we believe scriptural faith) is so tightly linked to love and obedience as to be nonexistent apart from them. Faith as knowledge and faith as trust cannot be disengaged and remain biblical faith. Calvinistic faith remains in the moment of conversion and does not enter into the warp and woof of life. Biblical faith is

[14]*The Epistle to the Hebrews* (Kansas City: Beacon Hill Press of Kansas City, 1959), p. 358.

[15]*Ibid.*

[16]Wesley was influenced by Luther to a great extent. It is said of Luther: The motivating force behind all Christian ethics is God's love. "Man receives God's love in faith and passes it on to the neighbor." Faith is active in love toward the neighbor. "Faith brings you to Christ and makes Him your own with all He has," then "love gives you to your neighbor with all that you have" (George W. Forell, *Faith Active in Love*, N.Y.: The American Press, 1954, pp. 100-101).

the total and new orientation to God which undergirds every moment of the Christian's life.

Leroy E. Lindsey says Wesley guarded himself against both Pelagian rationalism and Calvinistic antinomianism by understanding faith as a quality rather than as an entity.

> As an entity, faith could be isolated to a particular moment or a particular state of being. This is not so. Rather it is a quality that pervades all of our spiritual life, making possible and giving meaning to these experiences that constitute life. In this sense faith at any particular state of life would not differ in kind, but rather in degree, from the faith found in another state of life.
>
> The quality of faith that produces "faith unto righteousness" and results in the salvation of the individual is the same quality that leads the believer to sanctification.[17]

Morever, faith is the *condition to be met* in salvation, not the *cause* of salvation. The Calvinist practically robs faith of any meaning by lifting it out of the personal, moral acts of men. It seems that mild Calvinism scarcely avoids faith as works though that act of merit is limited to the solitary moment of the initial "acceptance" of Christ. For Wesley, faith was the precise opposite of works. It is ceasing from one's own works and placing one's absolute trust in Christ alone. This kind of faith is, therefore, a continuing new walk with Christ characterized by obedience and love. As Abraham's faith, which was accounted as righteousness, was demonstrated by obedience (Heb. 11:8), so our faith must exhibit the same characteristics.

To Wesley, faith was not an end in itself but the means to an end, namely, love. The whole of religion is love—not merely faith. The beginning of faith is the beginning of love. In Calvinism, it is faith that is perfect at the instant of justification. In Wesleyanism,

[17]*The Word and the Doctrine*, p. 287.

there are degrees of faith from the very weak to the perfect. As faith grows, love grows. But even weak faith can be true faith. We are to progress from faith to faith just as we are to progress in love. Wesley could speak of justifying faith and sanctifying faith. This is not two kinds of faith but young faith and perfected faith by which sanctification is entered. Some faith is weak (the faith of a servant), some is strong (that of a son), but all stages of faith please God and save from divine wrath and the guilt of sin.

"Believing" is always in the progressive present tense in the Greek, indicating a continuing responsibility on the part of the believer to maintain the new "walk of faith," which includes obedience and love (cf. John 1:7; 3:16-17, Acts 13:39; Rom. 10:9; John 20:3).

There is a real and necessary relationship between faith and good works and this can be established without making good works the condition of salvation. Wesleyanism does not teach that salvation is partly of God and partly of man. Faith is precisely the end of self-effort. But it is a continuing trust characterized by active love and obedience and subject to infinite development.

The crucial differences in the concept of saving faith, arising as they do out of significant differences of philosophy, lead to the practical differences in a concept of sanctification. A faith which is given to select persons by sovereign grace under terms of divine decree cannot lead to a dynamic concept of sanctification. It leads to a concept of unconditional eternal security which has no essential ethical elements in it. A faith which includes obedience and love, and is itself a dynamic and continuing response to God's grace, leads to the engagement of the whole man in total love to God and total ethical involvement with others. This is "perfect love" or holiness.

VI *Influence of the Wesleyan Doctrine of the Holy Spirit on Theology*

THE WORK OF THE HOLY SPIRIT

All the foregoing study helps us to understand better the tension existing between the Wesleyan and mild Calvinistic concepts of sanctification and the work of the Holy Spirit in the Christian believer. There is no desire here to intensify any antagonisms which may exist. The fact is that some Calvinistic people have contributed an exceedingly valuable emphasis to spiritual living. Relatively little literature on the Christian maturation process has been produced by the Wesleyan Arminian writers. Keswick writers, for instance, have filled the vacuum with much helpful material. However, there are emphases in Calvinistic and Keswick teaching that tend to undermine the biblical dynamic of sanctification.

Where much Wesleyan-Arminian teaching stresses the crisis aspect of sanctification to the neglect of the post-sanctification development and problems, the Keswickian tends to stress either the separation aspect (distinction between nature and grace and the conflict between them) or the growth aspect, to the neglect of the critical crisis aspect. Both groups tend to withdraw from any serious social responsibility and stress frequent retreats for personal spiritual life.

A study of the work of the Holy Spirit in the believer, as each group understands it, will reveal the significance of the tension between them. There ought not to be a theological tension because the Scriptures to which both cling hold both crisis and process in creative unity and encourage deep involvement in life. Our task, then, is to carefully examine the presuppositions of our respective views and to criticize them in the light of Scripture. Only an outline of this task can be attempted here.

The tension between the two theological traditions focuses in the psychology of personality. Generally the mild Calvinist and Keswick teacher understands human nature itself to be so corrupted by original sin that its effects are experienced inevitably in every man's thought, word, and deed, whether that man be a believer or an unbeliever. Springing up out of the unconscious are the sins which must be covered by "the white robe of Christ's righteousness."

Responsible Wesleyans also recognize the problems posed by the unconscious (or "below consciousness") life. Wesley himself was aware of this and said that "the most perfect have continual need of the merits of Christ, even for their actual transgressions. . . . For Christ does not give life to the soul separate from, but in and with, Himself. . . . Our perfection is not like that of a tree which flourishes by the sap derived from its own root but, like that of a branch, which, united to the vine, bears fruit, but, severed from it, is dried up and withered."[1]

Human Nature and the Victorious Life

While Wesleyan and Keswick people are equally concerned with the victorious life, the nature of that victory and the basis of it are different in each case and lead to quite different expectations of what the Christian life may produce. Individual emotional responses vary widely from person to person in all religious groups, and psychological reactions to life are not essentially determined by one's theology. But nevertheless, what one believes about himself as a human being and about God's grace has a bearing on the kind of Christian life one expects and hence experiences. The presence of the Holy Spirit may, and often does, surprise the Christian by a way of life totally unexpected. But one's theological "complex" may raise a barrier to that surprise that is sometimes difficult to overcome because faith for it is paralyzed by prejudice. If one believes that he must be victimized by sin, his conscience may not rise up to condemn him and his longing for holiness will die.

In other words, the incentive to holiness must be nourished by a faith that holiness is in the divine intention for fallible human persons. To understand the adaptability of the human psyche to the holiness that

[1] *A Plain Account of Christian Perfection* (Kansas City: Beacon Hill Press of Kansas City, 1966, reprint), pp. 52-53.

the Holy Spirit produces—yes, further, the essential human demand for this holiness which not only conforms to mental and psychic health, but is the only effective means to that health—is to clear the way to the experiencing of that life of victory.

What one believes about human nature and God's grace, then, will have a direct bearing on the kind of Christian life one experiences. One may have objective, joyous, outgoing, optimistic Christian faith, or else be too greatly concerned with the subjective aspect of personal emotional experience. A self-examining "retreat" complex like this and a withdrawal from society are usually accompanied by a rather pessimistic attitude toward life.

A third alternative is equally possible and somewhat prevalent, namely, an attitude which excuses oneself from the responsibility of spiritual victory and dynamic Christian service on the ground that no human being can live the life of victory and achievement which is lifted up as an ideal.

The mild Calvinist approaches this problem either by dividing the self into several parts, usually the flesh and the spirit, affirming a basic antagonism between these entities, or by sharply distinguishing in Christian experience between the abstract "in Christ" and the realistic "in ourselves." "In Christ we are sinlessly perfect, while in ourselves we remain unclean."[2] In either case the essential unity of the personality is ignored or denied. The Christian believer is not a "whole person" but divided to the core of his being. This is not only questionable theology but defective psychology.

The mild Calvinist, including the Wesleyan Calvinist, is sincerely concerned about Christian ethics and

[2]Edward Carnell, *Philosophy of the Christian Religion* (Grand Rapids: Wm. B. Eerdmans Publishing Co., 1952), p. 77.

spiritual victory and he emphasizes the Holy Spirit's role in the believer's struggle with his own sinful nature. But in this view, the Holy Spirit does not "cleanse" the heart, or change the heart. As the believer "s u r r e n d e r s" to the Holy Spirit, he is "possessed by" the Spirit. The Holy Spirit *controls, subdues, suppresses* the manifestations of the human nature. As the Holy Spirit possesses us, Christ reigns and "holds down" the sinful nature. "The beginning of the life of victory, and the soul of it, is that Christ is conqueror and we are overcome by Him. Christ must get the victory over us and in us."[3]

Christ's Obedience and Man's Righteousness

Much is made of Christ's passive and active obedience. Not only does Christ pay the penalty by His death for all our sins, past, present, and future, but His active life of obedience is transferred to our "account," so that our own "filthy rags" of righteousness may be covered and Christ's personal righteousness substituted.

The "substitution" motif is stamped on every part of this theology. Substitution looms so large that cleansing by Christ's blood is almost obscured and deliverance from sin practically denied. Substitution is a biblical truth, but its proper sphere of meaning must be exegetically determined lest its proper significance and relationships to other truths be lost. Holiness of character is never said in Scripture to be transferred from one person to another—nor is this possible. Christ's death is a substitute for our punishment but not for our holiness.

Great emphasis is placed on the "finished work of Christ on Calvary." But with the exaggerated and uncritical concept of substitution, there is a confusion

[3]J. Elder Cummings, "What This Teaching Is," *Keswick Week,* 1890, p. 40.

regarding what it is that is finished. Both justification and Christian character are considered to be included in the finished work of Christ which is applied to us, so that our personal righteousness and full sanctification are drawn unconditionally from Christ. In other words, not only our justification is "in Christ" but His own personal obedience becomes *my* personal righteousness without regard to the actual life I live or the sins I commit.

The weakness of this view is revealed by the use of such terms and expressions as "surrender to the Holy Spirit," "possessed by the Holy Spirit," "the death of self," "the transfer of Christ's righteousness to our account," "suppressing of the sinful nature," and suchlike. These terms point to an essentially superficial relationship of the Holy Spirit to man and to a psychologically unsound concept of human nature. The Scriptures are singularly free from them. *Not "surrender"* but "present"; not "possessed by" but "filled"; not *"suppressed" but "strengthened," are the New Testament words.* The concepts back of these contrasts are poles apart and are suggested by wholly different understandings of the nature of man and grace.

It is highly significant that "surrender," or its equivalent, is never used in the New Testament in connection with a relationship to the Holy Spirit. Never in the Bible are men said to be "possessed by" the Holy Spirit. "The spirit of the Lord came u p o n ["clothed," margin] *Gideon*" (Judg. 7:34). Similarly the Spirit "came upon" the prophets. The New Testament is even more specific. Men are "filled with," directed by, "strengthened with might by his Spirit in the inner man," etc., but never "possessed by the Holy Spirit."

Ironically, an overemphasis on the Holy Spirit to the neglect of the centrality of Christ can lead to a virtual loss of the proper concept of the Holy Spirit.

The Spirit's work is to reveal Christ, to press the claims of Christ on the human heart, to lead men to Christ, to glorify Christ (John 14—16). The Holy Spirit is Light. Light is to walk in, not to look at. The Holy Spirit's proper concern is Christ. This great truth must never be lost, lest we slip into the fanaticisms which have hurt the Church through history.

The Holy Spirit and Human Nature

The Holy Spirit is to be honored as God himself, but to honor Him most is to obey Him and to walk in the light He brings to us. Wesley was particularly careful of these matters. Among the very many terms he used for entire sanctification, never did he call it the baptism of the Holy Spirit or any like term because of the danger of seeking the Holy Spirit for some accompanying gift or emotion instead of seeking Christ and His will. Wesley's ethical insights are seen in the fact that he does not point us to the *gifts* of the Spirit but to the *fruits* of the Spirit. (See his sermon on "First Fruits of the Spirit.") The Scriptures' fine balance between the work of the Father, Son, and Holy Spirit must be maintained in our preaching and theology.

The New Testament does not teach the suppression of the human nature. Human nature must be dedicated, cleansed, and disciplined but never suppressed. Much is said about the role of the body in Christian experience. "Yield your bodies to [God] as implements for doing right: for sin shall no longer be your master . . ." (Rom. 6:13-14, *New English Bible*). "Present your bodies a living sacrifice, holy, acceptable unto God" (Rom. 12:1). "Your body is the shrine of the indwelling Holy Spirit . . . Honor God in your body" (I Cor. 6:19-20, NEB). "Wherever we go we carry death with us in our body, the death that Jesus died, that in this body also life may reveal itself, the life that Jesus lives . . . so that the life of Jesus may be revealed in this mortal body of ours" (II Cor. 4:10-11, NEB). "I shall speak so boldly that now as always the greatness of Christ will shine out clearly in my person . . ." (Phil. 1:20, NEB). In I Cor. 9:26-27, Paul speaks of keeping his body under ("buffetting" it), but this is an analogy of the training an athelete gives the body which he needs to bring him to victory (v. 25), not an analogy of a mystic trying to free himself from the restrictions imposed by his physical body.

The divided self is not the badge of the Spirit-filled Christian. A heart wholly loving God—a unified personality—is the badge. No part of the human psyche can be left out. The regenerating and cleansing effects of the grace of God go at least as deep now as the "heart," out of which "come the issues of life."

God requires all the powers of the self and human nature to be placed at the disposal of the Spirit (I Corinthians 12). He does not conquer or bypass the human self. He helps us to make Christ our Lord (I Cor. 12:3) and then each of us, with his own unique personality, is made "a limb or organ" (v. 27, NEB) of Christ's body, and the Holy Spirit manifests himself through us for some specific purpose of His own choosing. The passage used so often to prove that Paul held to a trichotomous view of human nature actually is his argument for a unified personality: "May God . . . make you holy in every part, and keep you sound in spirit, soul and body, without fault . . ." (I Thess. 5:23, NEB). The emphasis is not on the divisions of personality which the Thessalonians held, but on the unity which holiness establishes.

One of the steps to this spiritual wholeness is death to self or the "denial of self" (Matt. 16:24). This is a much different concept from "the death of self" of which some preachers speak. "Because the self dies there is room for Christ to live in us," comments Cummings in *The Victorious Life of Keswick*. Whatever he may mean by this, the impression is left that the self may step down out of the center of the personality to make room for another Self; or the self may even cease to exist. Such literalism tends to relax the sense of personal responsibility which is absolutely essential to wholesome mental health and moral character. The personality *is* the self. Remove the self and no personality remains.

The self with all its ransomed powers, strong in self-awareness and self-determination, must present itself to God, not passively, but as a "living sacrifice." The Wesleyan speaking of cleansing does *not* agree with F. B. Meyer when he says that human nature is *cleansed from self*. The New Testament teaches that it is the self itself that is cleansed from double-mindedness (Jas. 1:8) and sin (I John 1:9).

The self, as such, is not sin, but the self may be sinful. We cannot be cleansed from the self, but the self may be cleansed from its enmity against God. The self cannot abdicate its moral autonomy and selfhood. It cannot be suppressed. To attempt suppression is to tamper with the delicate balance of the God-made personality, and moral and mental disaster follows such attempts. But the self can be "strengthened with might by his Spirit in the inner man; that Christ may dwell in your hearts by faith" (Eph. 3:16-17).

The central and crucial point of this study comes to a focus in another weakness in the Wesleyan Calvinist's position, namely, the concept of a transfer of character from Christ to the believer, or that Christ's righteousness may substitute for my righteousness, or that Christ's obedience will be accepted by God in lieu of my obedience. In spite of the innumerable published statements to this effect, it is unlikely that any responsible theologian believes this literally. Righteousness and character are not commodities which can be passed from one person to another. They are qualities of the self which can neither be derived from another nor shared by another. Character, we repeat, *is the self* in dynamic encounter with life and God.

The only possible rationalization for this "character transfer" theory is (1) to protect the biblical truth that no man's personal goodness can commend him to God, and (2) that the Source and Cause of all righteousness is God. Under the Calvinistic concept of human nature, the only way to account for righteousness in man is to lift it away from the actual man so that it does not reside in him or touch him, yet permits him to rest in the security of a "standing" under the actual righteousness of Another.

The double standard which this creates is a serious matter and stands as one of the most significant distinctions between the Calvinistic and Wesleyan concepts of sanctification. In the Calvinistic tradition, sanctification is either (1) a gradual chipping away of the carnal nature and a gradual replacing of it with a spiritual nature; (2) an inevitable part of the predetermined security of the believer which may or may not touch moral character in this life; or (3) a "standing" in Christ which constitutes "perfection" while the believer in himself is unclean. In all these cases it is precisely the double standard that the Bible and the responsible Wesleyan reject as being the very condition of sin from which Christ died to save us. If men are not actually saved from sin, Wesley asked, from what does Christ save us?

Wesley said that through the new birth by the Holy Spirit a new life is accorded to the believer. This life will grow and develop toward perfection (see his sermon on "Salvation by Faith"). Wesley maintains that by salvation he means,

> not barely, according to the vulgar notion, deliverance from hell, or going to heaven; but a present deliverance from sin, a restoration of the soul to its primitive health,

its original purity; a recovery of the divine nature; the renewal of our souls after the image of God, in righteousness and true holiness, in justice, mercy and truth.[4]

Wesley contends that salvation by faith must not be reduced to a freedom from love and obedience. Salvation by faith is meaningless apart from the faith that works by love.

When we say, "Believe, and thou shalt be saved," we do not mean, "Believe, and thou shalt step from sin to heaven, without any holiness coming between; faith supplying the place of holiness"; but, "Believe, and thou shalt be holy; believe in the Lord Jesus, and thou shalt have peace and power: thou shalt have power from Him in whom thou believest, to trample sin under thy feet; power to love the Lord thy God with all thy heart, and to serve Him with all thy strength."[5]

The idea of a transfer of righteousness from Christ to man (or imputed righteousness) is the exact antithesis of the biblical concept of holiness. It relieves man of the necessity of any real heart change. Wesley said this was

a blow at the root, the root of all holiness, all true religion. . . . Hereby, Christ is "stabbed in the house of his friends, of those who make the largest professions of loving Him; the whole design of His death, namely, "to destroy the works of the devil," being overthrown at a stroke. For wherever this doctrine is cordially received, it makes no place for holiness.[6]

The Basic Difference

We cannot come any closer to the underlying gulf which separates the Calvinist and the Wesleyan. The

[4]*Sermons*, "A Farther Appeal."
[5]*Ibid.*, "Sermon on the Mount," I.
[6]*Ibid.*, "A Blow at the Root," 1762.

theory of God's sovereignty which requires a view of divine grace which cannot be resisted produces a concept of man who in turn must be unconditionally saved, if he is saved, either by divine decree or by virtue of his faith, without a true moral transformation.

The philosophy that supports unconditional personal predestination must of logical necessity reject the Wesleyan concept of sanctification. It will be discovered, moreover, that the arguments commonly heard against the Wesleyan doctrine of sanctification arise out of a Calvinistic philosophy even though the one who argues may claim he is not a Calvinist. The basic philosophy is as old as human thinking and can be traced back to Greek and Oriental roots. It is neither Hebrew nor biblical.

In the Wesleyan view, which is biblically based, not philosophically bound, sanctification is an essential element of salvation and must engage the total nature of man. Justification does not exhaust the gospel message. It is not the goal of the gospel. It is the first step toward the goal of full deliverance from the dominion of sin, love to God, and obedience to His law in this life. Sanctification is God's method of *healing a soul;* it is a means of renewing the corrupt nature of man. The renewal of man in the image of God becomes the end of religion. (See Wesley's sermon on "Original Sin.")

When the illogical attempt is made to base the Wesleyan doctrine of sanctification upon a Calvinistic doctrine of human nature, unresolved tensions result. Many people look for an automatic escalator to a holy life apart from the full response of their entire moral being. The coming of the Holy Spirit, to them, must mean freedom from temptation, freedom from all the weaknesses and extravagances of the demands of the body, freedom from themselves, freedom from the need of discipline, freedom from failure in Christian service, freedom from responsibility to one's fellowman, socially, spiritually, intellectually. But the coming of the Holy Spirit means the awakening of the total reserve of human nature, its cleansing from its double-mindedness, its radical dedication to God. It is a honing of the sharp edge of human energies and capacities in order to fulfill one's God-appointed mission in life.

The Holy Spirit and Christian Assurance

At no point in theology is the differing character of the two systems of theology under discussion more apparent in relation to sanctification than in the area of assurance relative to one's salvation. Just as the unconditional eternal security of the believer is the logical and necessary conclusion to the Five Points of Calvinism, so the Wesleyan practical logic (if it is logic in the formal sense) leads to a concept of conditional security. Strangely, the two systems charge each other with the teaching of insecurity. The Calvinist says the Wesleyan must live in fear lest his faith be inadequate and his "works" insufficient to assure salvation. The Wesleyan reminds the Calvinist that election is secret and none may know with absolute assurance that he is saved.

When the Calvinist is confronted by the realization of what kind of God his theology posits, he may extend his logic in another direction, not only to compensate for an unattractive view of God but also to build up a philosophy of assurance. If a predestinating God is to be delivered from the charge of injustice, and if His love is to be given serious consideration, why could He not elect to save everyone? Since no man can merit salvation, and salvation is only on the condition of God's decree, there is no philosophical or religious problem in presuming that God elects all men. This is called universalism. This theory is then able to take seriously the biblical affirmations about the atonement of Christ reaching to every man. The potential of universalism lies at the heart of Calvinistic philosophy.

Universalism cannot logically arise out of Wesleyan Arminianism because the latter does not postulate a God whose will is casual and hence restrictive of men's moral freedom. It cannot from its own premise give any assurance that all men will yield to Christ. Only irrational sentimentalism could come to such a conclusion.

Beginning with the concept of an absolutely sovereign God who is unable to tolerate any measure of a genuine contrary will in man, and placing alongside it the central truth that God is holy, we are logically driven to *unconditional particular predestination*. If we say, on the other hand, that God's central nature is love, logic drives us to *unconditional universal salvation*. Both stem out of a concept of God which permits no genuine moral freedom in mankind.

But between these two extremes lies the concept of God whose inner nature is holiness *and* love, both in perfect harmony and cooperation. It is surely to misinterpret Scripture to talk about a God whose attributes are in disharmony: His holiness against His love, His wrath against His mercy, His will against His desire.[7]

The Greek subjunctive tense indicating conditionality becomes a silent but inexorable barrier to the two Calvinistic views just mentioned. Sometimes we find the word "if" in the English to help us. More often the contingency is hidden in the Greek. Notice a few illustrations:

---

[7]See Wiley, *Christian Theology*, I, 365 ff., for an excellent analysis of holy love.

Man's Side (*conditional*)	God's Side (*promise*)
A. *Pardon, forgiveness, mercy*	
Isa. 55:7, "Let the wicked forsake his way, and . . . return."	"The Lord . . . will have mercy."
I John 1:7-9, "If we walk in the light . . . If we confess our sins."	"The blood . . . cleanseth."
B. *Assurance of acceptance*	
Matt. 11:28, "Come unto me, all ye that labour."	"I will give you rest."
John 6:37, "Him that cometh to me."	"I will in no wise cast out."
C. *Assurance of salvation*	
Rom. 10:9, "If thou shalt confess with thy mouth . . . and shalt believe [keep on believing] in thine heart."	"Thou shalt be saved."
D. *Assurance of sonship*	
John 1:12, "As many as received him . . . that believe [keep on believing] on his name."	"To them gave he power to become the sons of God."
E. *Assurance of eternal life*	
John 3:16, "Whosoever believeth [continues to believe] in him."	"Should not perish, but have everlasting life."
F. *Assurance of God's continued favor*	
Col. 1:23, "If ye continue in the faith."	"Present you holy and unblameable . . . in his sight" (22).

The Greek subjunctive is regularly used in relation to salvation. This is the tense which indicates possibility but also a condition—that we keep on believing. The subjunctive tense stands between predestined and moral choices. It opens up the possibility, but does not determine the result. It holds open the door to Christ, but it does not push anyone through the door against his will. All the barriers are removed between God and man, but man must use the powers God has given him to enter.

Another interesting fact is that all the verbs for believing are in the progressive present tense. Not simply one act of faith is enough, but a whole life lived in a continuing trust in God and obedience to Him is the New Testament wording.

This is the way the Bible avoids universalism (or the belief that everyone will be saved because Christ died for all men). The hyper-Calvinist solves this problem by saying that God elects certain ones to be saved and that Christ died only for those elect persons. The mild Calvinist seeks to solve the problem by respecting moral responsibility until one becomes a Christian (then moral responsibility ends and men cannot be lost). The Bible avoids both the logical and the moral problems of human thinking by holding men's moral responsibility within the framework of God's sovereignty. God is able to grant a definite measure of moral freedom in a way that does not limit His sovereignty. God says, "If you go this way, certain results follow. If you go the other way, another set of results will follow. You cannot escape the moral laws which I have predestined." Biblical grammar cannot be ignored in developing a Christian theology.

The very conditionality of biblical salvation, then, leads us into a very serious and profound understanding of sanctification. Assurance is not a static, amoral, even antinomian positionalism. Assurance is positive and dynamic, a life rooted in God, who cannot fail. It is a growing, deepening, expanding faith in Christ measured by a growth in love and obedience and which looks upward to Him, not backward to some past point, as important as this may be to the "entering in."

The true antithesis to Calvinism is the Wesleyan and (we believe) biblical concept of sanctification with its dynamic, life-involving meaning. Wesleyanism, unencumbered with the philosophy underlying Calvinism, finds the doctrine of sanctification not only biblical and practical but absolutely essential to salvation.

Dr. Neve reminded us earlier in this study that the doctrine of personal, unconditional predestination arose out of a need for inner assurance.[8] Personal predestination is the root of eternal security. The irony of the doctrine of eternal security is, however, that, divorced from its parent doctrine of election, it cannot provide assurance. Even linked to predestination one never can know whether he is elect or not.

Security which is divorced from election, as mild Calvinism holds it, rests on the quality of the faith of the believer. So one must constantly wonder, Was my faith genuine? A noted Calvinistic pastor once said: "Of course, if you continue in sin it is evidence that your faith *was* defective, you were never saved, for a Christian does not sin." This offers the questioning soul little consolation. Where does the doctrine of eternal security become assurance? What advantage does the doctrine have over the supposed fear in which a Wesleyan lives? On what ground does unconditional eternal security rest? On the other hand, what is the assurance of the Wesleyan? Does he rely on God or must he depend upon his own efforts? An outline of biblical teaching should suggest answers to these questions.

The Bible teaches two very clear things regarding the Christian believer: (1) There is absolute eternal security "in Christ"; and (2) The responsibility for continued obedience is binding on the Christian. The gospel requires much more than the "acceptance" of

[8]*Op. cit.,* I, 145.

Christ as a personal Saviour. In fact, this way of ex-
pressing the beginning of the Christian life is not only
unbiblical in terminology but unbiblical also in meaning. Who are we that have the right to "accept" Christ?
It is He who accepts us on His terms, n a m e l y,
believing. And believing is obeying Him. Moral
responsibility does not end with faith. Faith begins the
lifelong process of real, spiritual, obedient maturation.

There *is* security "in Christ." "Who shall separate
us from the love of Christ? . . . [nothing] shall be able
to separate us from the love of God which is in Christ
Jesus our Lord" (Rom. 8:35-39). "Neither shall any
man pluck them out of my hand" (John 10:28). "He
is able also to save them to the uttermost that come
unto God by him, seeing he ever liveth to make inter-
cession for them" (Heb. 7:25). He "is able to keep
you from falling" (Jude 24).

Let us examine these passages more carefully. The
Roman passage emphasizes the complete adequacy of
the lavish love of God for any and all human need.
But the need is occasioned by external dangers. The
will of the human heart to be kept is presumed. At
the same time it is affirmed that God's love is in-
exhaustible. That love does not end for *any* cause,
even the willful rejection of God on the part of man.
The same truth is expressed in John 10. It does not say
that no man can *escape* the Father's hand, but while
we are in that hand, no external power can touch us.
Hebrews 7 says that the condition for the "uttermost
salvation" is that we continually draw near to Him.
And the Jude passage about being kept from falling is
predicated upon the counsel in v. 32, "Keep yourselves
in the love of God."

Any serious view of moral responsibility must include the power of the believing Christian to reject,
as well as affirm, his loyalty to God. The sinner cannot
have a greater measure of the power of moral decision

than the Christian. Grace strengthens moral structure; it does not weaken it. In this opinion, the Bible gives full support. The whole Bible, and particularly the New Testament, gives repeated counsel and command to the believer to take very positive steps toward moral recovery. These r e q u i r e m e n t s are absolute. They are things the b e l i e v e r *must* do. God does not—and cannot—do them for him. Eternal destiny, not merely rewards, is at stake. God's forgiveness does not exhaust the obligations of the gospel; it begins the life of obligation. Notice a few of the passages:

"Reckon ye also yourselves to be dead indeed unto sin, but alive unto God" (Rom. 6:11); and, "Let not sin therefore reign in your mortal body" (v. 12); and, "To whom ye yield yourselves servants to obey, his servants ye are . . . whether of sin unto death, or of obedience unto righteousness" (v. 16). There is no *tertium quid,* or third way, between these e x t r e m e s for the Christian. The Christian (and it is to Christians that Paul is speaking) who yields his body to sin is headed for death. Paul's idea of security seems to be in a Christian's yielding in obedience to God.

The Christian's only alternatives are sowing to the Spirit or sowing to the flesh, according to Gal. 6:7-8. The consequence of this choice is either life or death. This law does not change for sinner or believer. This text is usually used for sermons to the unsaved, but Paul addressed this truth to Christians. This is significant.

The Heb. 2:3-4 passage is equally important to Christians, because it too is addressed to them, not to unbelievers. Lest we drift away from the salvation which has been provided, the writer warns solemnly against neglecting or ignoring it. If those who had been disobedient to the word of angels had met with due retribution, how shall we escape if we neglect the very word of the Lord himself, who has confirmed it by signs, miracles, and gifts of the Holy Spirit?

Not only are the above types of warnings given to the Christian, but direct commands are also given. A typical example is Eph. 4:22-24, "Put off" the old nature, and "put on" the new nature, which is created in truth and holiness. These commands are not gentle admonitions which we may or may not heed, according to our mood. Nor are they commands to carry on a lifelong chipping away of the carnal nature. The Greek aorist tense tells us this task is to be done decisively and wholeheartedly.

Christian assurance is based on at least two important truths. The first is the fact that *God's love prompts Him to surround us with every possible aid to meet every possible emergency.* God's love and power are a protective shield against the spiritual forces which oppress us and which we cannot see or even know about. We are encouraged to "be strong in the Lord" by putting on the "whole armour of God" to "be able to stand against the wiles of the devil" (Eph. 6:10-18).

There *is* security "in Christ." All of us experience testing times, times that shake the soul to its foundations. Sometimes the darkness makes us lose our grip on spiritual truths. Sometimes our faith is tested beyond measure. But then, in the depth and darkness, when we are helpless and alone, we begin to sense the presence of a Friend, the Friend who had never left us, the Friend who is able to reveal something more of himself in that hour than He could ever do when all was going well with us. It is difficult for a true Christian to backslide. To do so one must resist and reject all the gracious "lifelines" thrown to him and all the love surrounding him. In the ultimate test we experience the ultimate grace. We can never exhaust the forgiveness, mercy, love, and power of God. It is equal to every need.

The second important factor is *the nature of holiness*. Persevering in the faith is not the result of strength derived from the quantity of one's own faith, but the quality of one's love for God. To screw up the tension of one's own faith and rivet one's attention on it is to grasp the wrong source of help in times of need. We are not saved by the *strength* of our faith but the *Object* of our faith—Christ. We are linked together by mutual love.

Conclusion

Love is a positive force. Holiness is positive—a living, growing thing. In natural life we do not concentrate grimly on preventing illness but in strengthening the body that it may become healthy enough to throw off illness. We do not spend time and energy in trying to keep believing in our best friend. We love him and love takes care of the belief.

In our Christian life, the more we commit ourselves to God, the more we love Him and believe in Him. The constant "yes" to God weakens the "no" of the temptation to disobey God. We need not live under the strain of resisting sin and running away from it if we are running toward God and pressing more closely into His presence. Faith and love grow together. As faith grasps more and more of God's promises, and determination brings the self into conformity to God's will, love is perfected; and as love is perfected, faith is strengthened. "Perfect love casteth out fear" (I John 4:18). Love is the antidote for the fear of falling. Love trusts God. Love drives us to God where security is.

Everything necessary to a wholesome, strong, positive, Christian life is the meaning and content of holiness. Holiness is love. Love is not an abstract, imputed, unrealistic salvation which saves us in principle but not in fact. Love is precisely the grace of God acting and interacting on and with our essential selves, bringing every element of our beings and personalities under the mastery of the Lord Jesus Christ by the inner presence of the Holy Spirit. This stands in absolute contrast to salvation by divine decree which ignores the rehabilitation of the soul otherwise hopelessly lost in sin.

BIBLIOGRAPHY

BOOKS

ARMINIUS, JAMES. *The Works of James Arminius,* trans. Wm. Nichols. London: Thomas Baker, 1875.

BRANDT, CASPAR. *The Life of James Arminius,* trans. John Guthrie. London: Ward and Co., 1854.

BURTNER, ROBERT W., and CHILES, ROBERT E., eds. *A Compendium of Wesley's Theology.* New York: Abingdon Press, 1944.

CALVIN, JOHN. *Institutes of the Christian Religion,* trans. John Allin. Philadelphia: Presbyterian Board of Education, 1932.

CARNELL, EDWARD. *Philosophy of the Christian Religion,* Grand Rapids: Wm. B. Eerdmans Publishing Co., 1952.

COX, LEO GEORGE. *John Wesley's Concept of Perfection.* Kansas City: Beacon Hill Press of Kansas City, 1964.

FORELL, GEORGE W. *Faith Active in Love.* New York: The American Press, 1954.

GEIGER, KENNETH E., ed. *The Word and the Doctrine.* Kansas City: Beacon Hill Press of Kansas City, 1965.

HARRISON, A. W. *Arminianism.* London: Duckworth Press, 1937.

HODGE, A. A. *Outlines of Theology.* New York: A. C. Armstrong and Son, 1905.

McGIFFERT, ARTHUR CUSHMAN. *A History of Christian Thought.* New York: Charles Scribner's Sons, 1953.

MORGAN, G. CAMPBELL. *The Teachings of Christ.* Grand Rapids: Fleming H. Revell Co., 1913.

NAGLER, A. W. *The Church in History.* New York: Abingdon-Cokesbury Press, 1929.

NEVE, J. L. *A History of Christian Thought.* Philadelphia: The Muhlenberg Press, 1946.

ORR, JAMES. *Progress of Dogma.* Grand Rapids: Wm. B. Eerdmans Publishing Co., 1952.

OSBORN, G., ed. *The Poetical Works of John and Charles Wesley.* London: Wesleyan Methodist Conference Office, 1869.

RICHARDSON, CYRIL, ed. *Early Christian Fathers.* Philadelphia: Westminster Press, 1943.

SHEDD, WILLIAM. *Dogmatic Theology.* New York: Charles Scribner's Sons, 1888-94.

STRONG, AUGUSTUS. *Systematic Theology* Philadelphia: Griffith and Roland Press, 1907.

WARFIELD, BENJAMIN. *The Westminster Assembly and Its Work.* London: Oxford University Press, 1931.

WESLEY, JOHN. *A Plain Account of Christian Perfection.* Kansas City: Beacon Hill Press of Kansas City, 1966.

————. *The Works of the Rev. John Wesley.* 14 vols. Kansas City: Beacon Hill Press of Kansas City, n.d.

WILEY, H. ORTON. *Christian Theology,* Vol. I. Kansas City: Beacon Hill Press of Kansas City, 1940.

————. *The Epistle to the Hebrews.* Kansas City: Beacon Hill Press of Kansas City, 1959.

ARTICLES

ATKINSON, LOWELL, "The Achievement of Arminius," *Religion in Life* (Summer, 1950), p. 422.

BANGS, CARL. "Arminius and the Reformation," *Church History,* XXX (June, 1961), 7-8.

————. "Arminius: An Anniversary Report," *Christianity Today* (October 10, 1960), p. 18.

BARNHOUSE, DONALD GRAY. "Eight Things God Cannot Do," *Eternity,* IX (January, 1958), 27.

BELL, L. NELSON. "Righteousness," *Christianity Today,* II (June 9, 1958), 19.

CHILES, ROBERT E. "Methodist Apostasy from Free Grace to Free Will," *Religion in Life,* XXVII (Fall, 1958).

CUMMINGS, J. ELDER. "What This Teaching Is," *Keswick Week* (1890).

LADD, GEORGE E. "Justification," *Eternity.* IX (July 1958), 12.

"The Debate over Divine Election," *Christianity Today* (October 12, 1959).

VAN DER KROEF, JUSTUS M. "Calvinism as a Political Principle," *Calvin Forum* (February, 1950).